HATE/SMILE

THE GREATEST STORY

NEVER TOLD

Neal Studzinski

Table of Contents

Dedication

This book is dedicated to my parents David and Sandra Studzinski with whom I would be absolutely nothing without. I don't enjoy the prospect of you reading this book, but I know you eventually will. Thank you for everything you've done for me both monetary and mentally. Without your support, I don't know what I would do. You've helped me get back up on my feet so many times when I've been on my knees. I love you both dearly and I dedicate this book to you. Hopefully, it leaves some kind of mark that lives on well beyond us all.

In Loving Memory of

-Brian Barrett   1979-1997
-Reggie Barnard   1980-1998
-James Deel   1974-2011
-Bradley Marx   1980-2016

Preface

Normally, I don't read the Preface of books unless I've finished the book and I really liked it. I crave more information, so I go back to the beginning of the book and read the stuff I skipped over when I started reading it. It's humorous that I find myself writing one right now, actually. I wrote Hate/Smile for a few reasons. First and foremost, I wrote it to expose bipolar polar disorder to as many people as I can. It's mine for life although I've been episode free for a few years now. Secondly, I had put write a book on my bucket list and I'm now able to cross that off. Lastly, it's therapeutic for me to put these chapters of my life behind me. I find that documenting past events in my life allows me to close those chapters of my life for good.

Bipolar disorder affects 1% of the U.S. population, which is roughly 2.3 million Americans. It has kind of turned into a joke on social media. If someone is moody they may be called out as bipolar, but that's not really what it's about, being moody. Episodes can last months,. It's not really something that comes and goes all day, every day. I'd like to shed some light on bipolar disorder to the uninformed.

Every time I end a chapter it's like putting my stamp of approval on the way events happened and took place. I'm happy to share my stories with you using candor and honesty. It took me 5 years to write this book. So I really hope you enjoy it.

Acknowledgment

Ryan Hammer helped me with some of the stories in the book because he has a much better memory than I do.   Other than that, I don't really have anybody to acknowledge other than my Publisher, Contagious Publishing for having faith in me to deliver. We're going to get that second book out in record time!

Marshall Mathers III deserves some acknowledgment, because without him, you probably wouldn't have bought this book. His music inspires me to write. So I have to acknowledge the fact that he ignites a flame inside of me that makes me want to be better.

Prologue

Most of this story takes place in Detroit between the 1980's and 2010's. You may understand why I try to get away so often when you read my book. The following information is from <u>Wikipedia</u> regarding Detroit.

Detroit has gained notoriety for its high amount of crime, having struggled with it for decades. The number of homicides peaked in 1974 at 714 and again in 1991 with 615. The murder rate for the city has gone up and down throughout the years averaging over 400 murders with a population of over 1,000,000 residents. The crime rate, however, has been above the national average since the 1970s.

As of 2018, Detroit had the third highest murder rate among major cities in the United States after St. Louis and Baltimore and the 42nd highest murder rate in the world. The rate of robberies in Detroit declined by 67% between 1985 and 2014 while the rate of aggravated assaults increased. As a whole, however, the city's crime rate has decreased considerably from its 1980s peak in the 21st century

Chapter 1 – To Read or Not to Read

"*You think your pain and your heartbreak are unprecedented in the history of the world, but then you read. It was books that taught me that the things that tormented me most were the very things that connected me with all the people who were alive, who had ever been alive.*"
-                              James Baldwin

I felt high as a kite. At the moment, I felt like I could do anything in the world, I felt like whatever I did I would excel at it, everything felt good, and everything made sense. I was calm yet fast-moving... No, I was not taking drugs, as some of you might guess. I had a bipolar episode, the manic phase to be precise. Having bipolar disorder, and going through a manic phase is a strange experience. It is like chugging down several cups of black coffee and feeling highly energetic, doing anything and everything you think of. You feel like you can conquer the world. You feel unstoppable and your energy feels inexhaustible.

Your moods become disruptive. Your behavior shifts drastically and abruptly. Sometimes, when I have them, I feel there is no obstacle in front of me. Even if there is, I could easily and effortlessly overcome it. I feel that life is pretty easy, and all the fuss about it is overrated. However, this is just one side to the bipolar disorder. The other side that people experience is much more grim and difficult. When the manic phase ends, the depressive episodes creep their way in. The depression and hopeless state of mind becomes so severe and unbearable that many people end up wanting to take their own lives. They feel helpless despair. They do not want to be a part of this world.

At that moment, they feel so low that even the simplest tasks like getting out of bed and washing their face becomes an impossible task to do. They are unable to make any efforts of getting out and resuming their life, as any other person would. People who experience this and suffer from the disorder fall on the extreme end of the emotional spectrum, while those, like me, experience mania as I described above. That is just how the disorder works. Once you have it, there is no cure, just treatment to control the symptoms.

But this also makes one realize that it is not a one-size-fits-all disorder. Some of you reading this might have experienced this at least once in your life, or maybe you have been diagnosed with bipolar disorder, but your symptoms may be different and so, you might not be able to exactly relate to my episode. But there could also be some of you who would not be able to relate at all despite suffering from bipolar disorder.

But don't stress, this is largely because bipolar disorder is a vast disorder that cannot be categorized or summarized entirely. There are different ways of feeling and experiencing mania of the bipolar disorder, and I will explain all of that later. However, for now, just know that even if you cannot entirely relate, or at all, what you experience is still valid and real.

My reason for mentioning all of this is to tell you guys that I have been struggling with this disorder for a while now. But, thankfully, I have learned not only to live with it; but function normally. In fact, functioning normally might be an understatement, I have not only survived it, but I have also thrived and lived my life to the fullest. And this is my story. So, stick around and you will soon find out.

Anyway, enough about that. I am going to talk to you about my book. Man, it's been a while since I have been thinking about it. It was on my bucket list after the idea came to me during a manic episode, and this is one of the things that I can finally cross off of it. Do you know the feeling that you get when you cross things from a bucket list, that sense of accomplishment, the satisfaction and pride you gain? Yeah, I felt the same as I struck out that part. But I digress. So, if you're wondering what the point of this book is or why I am going on about bipolar disorder, let me just cut to the chase and dive right into it.

Having bipolar disorder is challenging, to say the least. To be fair, having any kind of mental illness is difficult. It takes a toll on you and can really mess with your life. It changes you as a person. It not only affects you, but leaves long lasting consequences on those around you if not treated properly and in time. Of course, I know this applies to diseases of the body as well, and I am in no way downplaying the suffering of fellow cancer patients or any patient for that matter. What I mean is, there is already stigma around having a mental illness. People don't really know what life looks like for a person who has such a disorder. In fact, in some places around the world, mental illnesses are still a taboo and believed to be non-existent. Either that, or they are not taken seriously. So, I thought about sharing my story in hopes that when you read it, you will understand the constant inner battles people with mental illnesses deal with, and the things they go through in every step of their life. While you attempt to understand, I hope it helps you empathize with those around you who may be struggling with a mental illness. I also hope that it helps you relate to people like us, and we break this stigma around mental illnesses. The point is not to separate us from those who have been fortunate enough to be neurotypical. We don't want to feel alienated; instead we just want acceptance. We, too, are human beings, just like everyone else. All of us are fighting a tough battle that others may have no idea about, and we need to try to make life easier for not just us, but everyone around us.

As repetitive as it is, this book is not actually about bipolar disorder. Sure, it is a recurring theme and it will come up again and again, but this book is about my life; how I grew up in a regular family and lived a regular, normal life that most people do. Of course, I had my ups and downs. Who doesn't? But it wasn't anything out of the ordinary, at least not in my early years. I had a loving family and good friends, I performed average in school and didn't have any problems that worried me constantly.

However, I can't say the same as I grew up. Things changed, definitely, and they changed fast. I mean, my battle with bipolar is definitely out of the ordinary. But I did some other unusual stuff too…and did not always get away with it, as you will soon come to discover. Word of advice, I don't suggest you take inspiration and do the same things I did and get into trouble, thinking you'll be okay. This is not one of those books. Maybe you might not be okay and could get into some serious trouble. Perhaps I just got lucky, and you might not. Who knows!

So the first chapter, I have pretty much covered above. I won't repeat myself too much, don't worry. The book is not dull, I promise, it's far from boring but I have to establish the story and build it. It will talk about my early days. Man, I really did beat the odds of coming into this world. It's incredible how that happens. No, I am not talking about how the odds of sperm swimming into the egg are one in a million, or whatever the odds are. I am talking about actually beating the odds, but once again, I'll talk about that later.

I had my fair share of fights and punishments, especially with my siblings. I mean, I was the youngest of three boys. What can you expect? The youngest brothers are the most teased. It's not as if I grew up with perfect siblings or the ideal family. Who does, really? They don't exist. I'll also tell you about the quirky side of my family. We have so many quirks. I guess that is what sets us apart from the rest. We also have a lot of information about my great grandparents. I think not too many children know about their great grandparents. They were some extraordinary people. And I'm not just saying that because they were my grandparents. But, I guess I do have a long way to go before I get there.

Moving on, I will tell you about the time I became friends with the nephews of Jack White. Some of you may not know him, but he is a world known famous musician. I also became friends with Eminem before he became Eminem. None of us knew we would have a world-famous star walking amongst us. Man, life can be full of surprises, right? You never know that acquaintance or friend from high school could soon, in a few years, be one of the most famous people in the world! We were actually really close to his roommates and him in high school. Then life happened, as it so often does.

I also had a party side. You wouldn't guess that if you saw me back then. I think my friends might have noticed that, though. The partying did not alter my life too much, thank God. It did a little bit, but not in a wrong way, anyway. I mean, did you hear of party people who grow up to be addicts. Some of them either take their own lives because of an overdose. Some of them are so high while driving they don't know what is coming their way. They end up hitting someone in the opposite car or getting themselves killed. I did not have such episodes in my life, although I do have a few DUIs.

I fell in love with it. It was everything it was supposed to be…and more, but also less. I had crushes from a young age, who doesn't? But I also had the opportunity to find love. I faced heartbreaks and learned to become resilient. All the while, I was also battling bipolar episodes. But I would not change that for the world.

I have also gone to jail. I know. I know what you are thinking, I did not murder anyone. I promise! I wasn't in it for too long of time, though. And it's not as if I will ever go back. But I do have the experience of going to jail a couple of times. It was different, in a word. It turned me around and shaped me. But to be fair, there are a lot of incidents in my life that have shaped me. So I can't say I regret any of them too much. Never regret a thing, is what I mean. Incidents happen in your life to shape you. Just ride them out.

So I battled through bipolar disorder and became my own cheerleader. It was satisfying to be able to depend only on myself. I hope those of you who are battling your demons and feel that you are alone can take some encouragement from my story. You will get through the problem, and you will come out stronger. You are enough for yourself, and you have what you need to come to the other side. No matter how daunting the problem is, the solution is in yourself. Just dig deep down to find it.

That is the story of my book. The above was just a summary of the things I have spoken about in great detail in the upcoming chapters. I hope you can relate to it, and I hope it helps you on your journey to self-discovery. Take lessons from this book and apply them to your life. You might be able to make peace with yourself, your surroundings, and your family members the way I have.

A little side story to keep you entertained, and also because ending the chapter like this did not seem fitting to me. Before I go into too much detail, there are just some things I want to tell you about myself and the generation I belong to. So, I was born in 1979. We are the middle children of the ages, so to speak. The experts say we belong to Gen X, but some people say we are part of the Millennials. The most hated and entitled class—according to the generational experts anyway. So we grew up with this feeling of not belonging to a particular group. We were given names by these experts such as "Xennials," "The Lucky Ones," and how can I forget the "Generation Catalano"? No label has ever stuck, you know, although I would say Xennials sounds pretty cool.

Anyhow, our generation is this left out middle child who did not really belong to a group and are always searching to be a part of something. Thus, they have identity crisis and go on with their lives trying hard to fit in or belong somewhere by trying out things from different generations. I might be exaggerating a bit here. I might have landed on something and you can now relate to something you could not put into words before. But you get the point. We were that part of the population who had the weirdest relationship with technology and the internet. We came to be of age just as things were slowly transforming, we found ourselves in the middle of the modernism era and the development of technology, while the art and pop culture was slowly taking off. The world would never be the same.

We were well into our teens; some were young adults when computers started to become more mainstream. We were already proficient at them when some middle-class families were just beginning to afford these giant PCs. We were the first generation that was growing up to understand just how computers worked. It was also unlike the Millennials, who had intimate knowledge about how the technology was used from a very young age. Come to think of it, I believe we deserve being separated from the other generation. We deserve having another name because, I mean, we have a very different experience from the Millennials and Generation X. It's not fair to lump us together. They cannot identify with us. Just as we cannot identify with them. Come to think of it, maybe that is the reason why I did not get along with my brothers. Particularly my middle brother. Man, the things he would do to me. Oh, the stories I can narrate, and I probably will. But you'll have to wait until the next chapters to read about our relationship. It was interesting, to say the least.

You might be wondering why I am talking about the different generations. I mean, you're probably saying, 'didn't you tell us that this was not a book about information; it was about your life?' And yes, you're right. I was only telling you about the different generations to explain to you about the kind of world I grew up in and the kind of options I had in front of me to entertain myself. I want to give you guys a better background about who I am and where I come from, to put things into context. Another reason is to make you marvel over how things change as life evolves and how rapidly they do so —a common theme of the book, by the way. But I cannot help reminiscing. The "you've got mail" voice I used to hear would fill me with anticipation every time I logged into AOL. Whose mail did I receive? What did it say? The AOL icon circled while it opened my mail. I remember feeling impatient and excited about who just sent me mail. In this day and age, we are so used to instant gratification we forgot the value of waiting. Everything is so easily available, and while that has done wonders for the advancement of the world and brought people closer despite thousands and thousands of miles of physical distance, it has taken away the anticipation. I remember how painfully slow the dial-up connection would be, and how my eyes would be fixated on it, waiting for connection. I used to wait through that and looked forward to the time when I would be able to read the mail. Those were the simpler times, and the innocently happier ones.

I am proud of the generation that we belong to. We are supposed to be the go-betweens, the individuals who are the most resilient ones in the chaos that is happening around us. We are the misfits who found our place despite the odds. This is also a testament to my life. I am the resilient one, and I stood firm in the face of adversities. No matter what came my way, I stood my ground and faced it in any way I understood best to my knowledge, and I persevered. This is why I am alive today and can narrate to you my life stories. I guess the generation I was born into did play a part in shaping me also. Anyway, now begins my life and my story. So stick around; you might enjoy reading all this. Who knows, you might even learn something valuable about yourself. You might see yourself in my story! That's it for today, folks; see you on the other side!

Chapter 2 – The Family Tree and the Good Ole' Days

"Childhood is like being drunk, everyone remembers what you did, except you."*
-   Anonymous

In the previous chapter, I mentioned how I know so much about my ancestors. It is really unusual, considering that most people don't even remember their great grandparents' names; unless they were important individuals in history. The family tree for most families does not go back for so many generations. That is not the case with me. I can trace back my ancestry all the way to the 1700s. Yes, that is how well kept the records of my family are. But I know that would become too boring for you, so I will not delve into it. I am just going to tell you the most interesting stories. I promised I would not let my book get boring, so here it is. I would credit this to my paternal grandmother, Rita Danbert who has a pretty interesting family background. I'll make sure that I will stick to that. So get on board.

John Danbert was my fraternal 3rd great grandfather and he was born in 1844 in Switzerland. I guess that means I have some European blood in my family, but then again, it is difficult to find individuals that are not of European heritage—thanks in part to the colonization. Anyway, John Danbert immigrated to the United States when he was very young and lived in Flint, Michigan for a number of years. He turned 21 in 1862 and started working as a gas fitter in Detroit. When the Civil War broke out, he was one of those individuals who enlisted with Company D, a 24th Michigan Infantry under Col. Henry Morro. He fought well in the battle and managed to escape injury in the Battle of Gettysburg. If you think that is the worst he faced, you are wrong. Three years after he signed up, he had his left leg blown off at the Battle of Hatches Run on February 7, 1865. Imagine the pain and horror that he must have had to go through. He was lucky. He was the only soldier in his platoon of six men that survived this battle. It's not as if things got easier after that. For seven hours, my 3rd great grandfather lay on the battlefield in that position just waiting for his leg to be amputated. Can you imagine the agony he must have gone through? After the amputation, he rode an ambulance for over twelve miles of corduroy (logs laid side by side transversely to make a road surface). This incident is even recorded in history in the following words:

"A solid shot passed directly under sergeant Augustus Pomeroy, which stunned him and covered him with mud. The same shot ricocheting, killed Sergeant George H. Canfield and George Wallace, both of Company I; wounded Sergeant Walter Morley of D and took a leg off of John Danbert of D." (Curtis p. 292)

My 3rd great grandfather was discharged from the hospital and the army on June 8, 1865. Since he was missing a limb, he was eligible for a pension and he was also eligible for a new leg. In 65 years, he had received three legs and still possessed (1932) the first leg that was issued to him. My 3rd great grandfather died at the age of 89 and at the time, his pension was $100 per month. This was a definite boost because during the war he earned only $13 per month. He died in 1932 and was the only war veteran living in Canada at the time and was one of only fourteen war veterans still living from the American

Civil War. My 3rd great grandfather is the picture of resilience. Standing strong in the face of adversities was one of his greatest gifts, I believe, and one that I seem to have inherited because I battled bipolar disorder in the same way too.

He married Clara Sussana Karrer who was also from Switzerland. They had my 2nd great grandfather John Danbert II. They had eight children, but for some reason, he left behind his entire family and moved to Buffalo, NY before moving to Canada. He never claimed these children, despite having a good business and pension. When he reached Canada, he took a second wife, Barbara Teufel. They had two daughters and a son. He was an admirer of Abe Lincoln and proudly cherished the time he once shook Honest Abe's hand while in Washington DC. He admired Lincoln to the point where pictures of Lincoln adorned his entire home. According to him, "Lincoln was a good man in spite of any statements to the contrary". Tells you something about his mentality, doesn't it?

John Danbert II, the son of John Danbert was born in 1866 and he became a farmer in Northern Michigan. He married Anna Bertha Flemming in 1889 and she gave birth to my great grandfather John August Danbert in 1900. John Danbert II, died later in life, tragically when at the age of 74, he went to Hoeft State Park in northern Michigan to pick berries and never returned. His remains were not found either—a tragic end.

His son John August Danbert only managed to reach the 7th grade before he was forced to quit to help his family financially. He married Teresa Wisniewski in October 1920 in Michigan. They had three boys and two girls. One of them was my fraternal grandmother, Rita Danbert who was born in 1926.

My paternal grandfather's lineage can't be traced back very far. My 2nd great grandfather, Julius Studzinski spent his life in Poland, but his son Frank, who was born in Poland, immigrated to the US at the age of 26, in 1911.

He was a trade smith by profession and so, he continued to do that here in the US. My great grandfather Frank married his first wife Pauline Dombrowski on August 21, 1919, and she died just two years after marriage. He took a second wife named Mary Malelskre who gave birth to four kids, including my grandfather Edmund in 1925 in Detroit where he was raised.

He was another veteran in our family as he, along with his brothers, fought in the Second World War. When he returned to Detroit, he joined the Detroit Police Department. Do you know the famous 1967 Detroit riots? They were a nightmare. Yes, my grandfather was part of the police department when that happened. It lasted for 5 days resulting in the death of 43 people. There were also 1189 who were injured, 7200 arrests, and more than 2000 buildings that were destroyed in the process. It had gotten so bad that the army tanks were driving down the roads. The police had to step back and let the rioters do whatever they wanted to. But my grandfather's work was exemplary. He had many arrests to his name. He decided to retire from the department in 1972 and after 25 years of service, he took a job as a janitor at NBD bank.

My grandmother, Rita Danbert worked at Chrysler while my grandfather was away during the war. When he returned, she became a homemaker that raised four children: Janice, my father David, Thomas, and Paul. She had really bad arthritis and this meant that she could not take up a lot of the work that was to be done by hand. Thankfully, my grandfather returned in one piece so she was not forced to do too much in that condition.

My mother, Sandra, lost her father when she was young. She had a tough life as her dad died when she was 19. It was pretty sudden. His name was Edward Wojcik and he worked at Chrysler on the assembly line. He was going about his business one day when he had a sudden heart attack. There were no warning signs or anything. He was shoveling snow and suddenly, he was on the ground withering in pain. He was rushed to the hospital where he was treated and was showing signs of recovery. Fate, however, had other plans and before he could be discharged, he suffered another heart attack. This time, it was so severe that he could not survive. He died on Valentine's Day leaving behind his wife and children.

Things were harder on his widow and my grandmother, Jean. She had lost her husband and her mother the same week. Imagine the emotional turmoil she was going through as she tried to bring her family together. What was worse was the financial situation that the family was going to be facing. Things were not so progressive back then and despite the fact that my grandfather had worked at Chrysler for 27 years, his widow was not entitled to his pension. There was no concept of a vested pension at the time. So effectively, my grandmother received nothing at all. Not one cent. I think the stress drove her to illness because a couple of years down the road, she became so ill that she could not work at all. She also developed breast cancer, which was another blow for my mother who had already seen one parent go. My grandmother counted on my mother for several years to help her with her finances. My mother could not abandon her so she did what was required of her. She became her pillar of strength.

Do you know what the funny thing about this story is? My parents grew up just three streets apart from each other. They were both in Detroit but my mother lived on Binder while my dad lived on Norwood. However, they never met one another until they were in their early 20s. I guess that is weird because it was clear that the two were destined to be together. I think since my parents were three years apart, it kind of makes sense that they did not meet until they were older. The two of them met when my mother was 25 and my father was 22. They met at a bar and after dating for a short period, they got married in July 1973. It was a large wedding and one of the happiest occasions of my parent's life.

About two years after the wedding, my parents bought a house on Kensington Street in Detroit. This was in April 1975 and it was two years after the birth of my oldest brother, Scott. Then, Justin was born in 1976 and just three years later, in 1979, my parents welcomed me.

I was a bit of a surprise. Actually, a shock would be a better way to describe my arrival into this world. Remember how, in the earlier chapter, I spoke about how I beat the odds of coming into this world? Well, here is the full version of the story. Right after my brother, Justin was born, my parents decided that my mother would get an IUD implant. My mother had one inserted in August 1978. You know what an IUD is like, it's a small T-shaped plastic device that is wrapped in copper. It contains hormones and the IUD is inserted into the uterus and is used as a contraceptive, just in case you did not know. Modern ones can stay in place for 10 years and it is supposed to be highly effective when it comes to contraception. My point in telling you all this is that despite all the protections my parents took to make sure Justin would be their last kid, I came into this world. I beat the odds of contraception and my mother got pregnant again.

I am now part of the 1% in their 99% ratio to slip under the radar and defeat the IUD. I picture myself fighting off the other sperm as you know at the beginning of the movie 'Look Who's Talking'. That is the picture that automatically flashes in my mind every time I tell someone about the odds I beat to get here. The tadpoles are the sperm that are fighting around to be the one to break out and fertilize the egg. Of course, there are some days that I am so grateful I slipped through the walls of the uterus. Other days, not so much. Like I said, life is about ups and downs and we get to experience everything in between.

So, I was born on Memorial Day in 1979 when my mother was 31 years of age. I came into this world at 6:08 am and my weight was 7 lbs. 10.5 oz. I was 20 ¾ inches tall, so you can say that I was a healthy baby. My mother was worried that the IUD would end up inside of my head or my body and create problems for me. It could have certainly caused serious brain damage which would have impacted my life. I am still not sure, to be honest. There are days when I feel that there was some damage. I felt this especially around the time I was diagnosed with bipolar disorder. The doctors checked the x-ray of my mother's womb and were unable to find anything. The worrying part was that they could not even find the copper piece. No matter how many X-rays they ran, they were just never able to locate that IUD. It was like it did not exist at all. They did not even find it in me, which was a relief to my mother. At least that meant there was no damage. We never actually managed to find that thing, my mother assumed that it must have fallen out somehow and she was never able to solve the mystery. It doesn't really matter, the important thing is that it is not in either one of us.

A child will sometimes ask their parents if they were a mistake or unplanned. Every time a parent is asked that you should see the look on their faces, especially when the child is unplanned. The parents try to cover it up by saying something like, "You weren't a mistake, you were a surprise," anything to appease the child. I believe that in my case it is both. It was a pretty good plan that went wrong, but it turned out to be a surprise in any case. So all's well that ends well, right? Then, to top it all off, after coming to terms with the fact that they would become parents once again, they hoped to have a baby girl. I mean, I get their point of view. They already had two boys and now that they were having another one. Ideally, it would be that they have a girl. It would complete the family, so to speak. But fate once again intervened.

I was born and they named me Neal Aaron. My mother told me that if I was a girl, they would have called me Amanda Jill. It's a beautiful name, I suppose. I came home from the hospital five days later on June 4, 1979, at

12:30 pm. We had a babysitter back then, Patty was her name. She was there to help my mother with my brothers and myself. She was a gem of a person who was a bit of a scatterbrain…I'll tell you more about her later. Around 10 days after I was born, I was taken to my pediatrician, Dr. Alpern, for a first exam. He had to cauterize my umbilical cord because it wouldn't come off. I am so grateful that I don't remember anything about that scene. I am sure I must have been crying and screaming because of the pain. He was a nice man, who also treated my heat rash.

As a baby, I gave my mother a tough time. Who doesn't, if we were to think about it? I remember reading my mother's entry into my baby book. She had written "Dislikes water and baths. Likes being talked to and walked". This was just when I was six weeks old. I think I was developing a personality from that time and I was showing it to my family. Since my parents were churchgoers, I was baptized. The church where I was baptized was St. Clare of Montefalco church which is located on Mack Avenue in Grosse Pointe Park. The ceremony was carried out by Father John Burkhart. One interesting thing came from this entire event. My mother chose her brother, Gilbert, and his wife, Carolyn to be my godparents. At the time, there was a rift that was going on between my mother and her brother and this had been going on for a long time. I think, the kind of person that my mother is, she wanted to make amends. So she extended the olive branch to him by making him my godfather. I was the peace offering, I suppose. But I am so grateful that nothing ever happened to my parents. I would not want them to step in and fulfill their role as my godparents. I just would not.

Time went on and I started to grow up. I was turning into my own person. I said my first word when I was only 9 months old. "Da da". At the age of 1, we went to St. Petersburg Beach in Florida to visit my grandma Jean. I don't recall much of the event, or actually anything at all. I think I was too young to remember all this, but I guess it was fun. That is what my mother tells me anyway. And I agree with her.

We were also one of those families that celebrated Halloween. It was my second Halloween and it was a couple of months after the trip to Florida. I was dressed up as Robin Hood and my mom says I looked really cute. I don't have any pictures lying around but I take her word for it. Growing up, I think I was loved, protected, and nurtured by my parents. For the most part anyway. It was a different time to grow up in. What is considered to be nurturing then isn't considered nurturing today. I'll elaborate more on this later. My parents did try to have a proper family. They even wanted to celebrate every occasion as evidenced by the birthday parties, Halloween, and 4th of July events that I have attended and have extensive photographs.

So I want to talk to you about Patty. I mentioned earlier that she was a bit of klutz. She was also really absent-minded, but she was a good person. My mother hired Patty when she was only eighteen years old. She babysat for my brothers for a little while before I came along. She looked after me for 5 years and had her quirks. For instance, she would invite her entire family over to the house a day after my mother had gone grocery shopping. It's like her family was feeding off our food. They had access to cheese, rolls, meat, and sandwiches. This food, as you might have guessed by now, was not for her family. It was for my brothers' who returned home from school and were effectively starving. Well, you know how young boys are. They eat everything and always want more. It's like they have bottomless pits for stomachs. My brothers were really no different. She was an amazing babysitter though, and my mother never said anything to her because of that. But it also shows you what kind of a person my mother was. She was always looking to settle matters quietly without creating a scene. That was also why she extended the olive branch to her brother by making him my godfather.

Patty wasn't smart…at all. But I still loved her. She had a pure heart I think, which did not prevent her from breaking lots of my mom's wedding crystal in the dishwasher. She also smashed the coffee pot into the refrigerator, I mean who effen does that? But you get what I mean when I say she was a bit of a klutz. She babysat my brother, Scott for a long time, and in his birthday card she wrote, "Happy Birthday, Scoot!" I am chuckling as I write this story. I wonder where she is now. The event became something of a joke because my mother, to this day, teases my brother by calling him Scoot. But that is Patty for you.

The amazing thing was that she knew how to play. Man, it was as if she got me or that we had some kind of a connection. She could color with me for hours without getting bored. You know how some babysitters get bored and let the kid do whatever he wants? Patty was not like that. She was so invested in me. In us, actually. I remember, this one time my mother returned home from work pretty early. She walked into my room and saw that Patty and I were playing house. I mean, we were really playing house. I was the daddy and she was the mommy and we had a little baby who was a doll. There was no actual baby, of course.

All in all, I would think I had a wonderful time with her. Later on, Patty started to bring her niece, Ann Marie and she became my first best friend. I have good memories of her too.

Time flew by, and I grew up as one does. We also went for a vacation to Niagara Falls in 1981. I think we took a family vacation almost every year. In 1982, I turned three and I remember we had a birthday celebration. I don't remember the whole event, of course, but snippets of it. It was in the backyard of the Kensington house. There was Gilbert, Carolyn, Grandpa, and Grandma. I remember some noise and a bit of imagery of the garden which was all decorated. My parents went out of their way to celebrate our birthdays, I think. I also got gifts, my mom told me. The one I remember was a red tricycle. Don't recall the rest of it.

In the same year, I went to the zoo and rode my first elephant. I think I might actually have been crying my head off, but I think I enjoyed the ride, that is what my parents tell me. I think this was also the year I saw my first fireworks. We went to our family friends, the Hills' house in Tennessee and watched them light off some fireworks. I remember how they lit up the entire sky. Again, that is just a snippet of the memory I have. We celebrated Halloween and this time, I was dressed as Superman. My brother Scott was The Greatest American Hero and Justin was Batman. That is about it for the year 1982, I think.

I think this was the time of my life which really started to shape my perceptions about the world. I also faced bullying at the hands of my brothers which was probably the reason for this change in perception. I was 4 at this time and my playmates were Hillary and Dougie Jennings from down the street instead of Patty. I learned to ride a bike in July of 1983. My father took the training wheels off my bike and away I went. I was at the stage where I could not use the brakes well. So I kept going on and on and rode right into a tree right across the street from Hillary and Brian's house. It was in full view of the boys, who were playing football, which kind of made me embarrassed. And you know what that is like, to be a young boy where you already feel shy and you see some older boys who happen to view your most embarrassing incident. My brother Scott and Brian were the same age and Hillary and I were close to the same age, so we spent a lot of time together. They were playing football in the front yard when I crashed into the tree. But thankfully, I did not get hurt. But I was still a bit embarrassed.

That Christmas, my parents gave me a trophy which stated that I was the "Youngest Bike Rider in History," and I believed them. I was only four years old at that time. Besides, I had always envied my brothers who were always receiving trophies for soccer or bowling, so I wanted them too. I still have it, you know. It is in my basement and I absolutely love it. Some kids cannot ride a bike until 10, nowadays which is really sad. Chloe, who lived across the street, was unable to ride a bike until she was 7 or 8. I'm glad my parents pushed me into learning this stuff earlier.

It was also around that age I started to get growing pains in my feet. That is what the doctor called them. The pain was unusual and is difficult to describe, but it hurt a lot. The doctor did not really help me much at all. He was full of useless ideas that did not make sense to implement so I ignored him. I remember that sometimes the pain got so intense that the only way I was able to get some relief was to run ice cold water on my feet. That numbed the feet so I could not feel anything. My dad was a bit creative and he was always looking for ways to alleviate the pain. He once told me that I should run hot water on my feet and then sit in a blanket. Needless to say, it did not work and I grew out of it eventually.

During this time, I was also dealing with Scott and his large group of friends. They would come over to the house on Kensington and would try to pick on me. They would call me names, taunt me, and upset me every chance that they got. It irritated me, I did not want to be subjected to their bullying. They were six years my senior and still bullied me. I mean that tells you more about them than about me. They were so much bigger than me and I could not help myself in any way. That frustrated me to no end. There were times when the taunting got so unbearable that I had to chase them around the yard. I would pick up anything that I could find and run after them. It could be a stick or even a belt from my father's closet. That was how frustrated I felt.

I remember this one time, this friend of Scott's, Matt must have caught me on a bad day. I remember I threw a steak knife at him and it stuck in his leg. Yes, I know what you are thinking. But I had no other choice. No belt or stick would make any difference. But for some reason, this time it worked and he backed off, at least for that day. This was a victory for me and I felt that the only way I had to deal with them was to attack them. I needed to fight for myself in the only way I knew how.

This continued. It was either one or the other of my brothers who were constantly taunting or teasing me. I would threaten to break their trophies or something else that they valued. Like Justin loved his teddy bears and I took them. It was a defense mechanism, I think. I needed to shut them up. I could only take on the taunting so much.

You may be wondering where my mother was in this whole scene? Well, my brothers started to involve her. But she heard my brother's side of the story. The day I attacked Matt with a knife, my brother called my mother at work and told her. She told me over the phone that I would be getting four with the belt when she got home. Yup, there were times when I felt that I could not rely on anyone. I could not look to my parents for support even in the face of bullying. She came home that day and gave me four. It was as if no one was on my side.

I had my own quirks. When I was too young to buy anything for anyone, I used to steal my brother's stuff and hide them just before Christmas. They would be looking for the item and I would pretend that I had not seen anything. I was sneaky in a way. Come Christmas morning, and they would get it back as my gift to them. I used that move for a long time and it was clever, in a way. You have to give me that. I tried to make the most of my situation, and I think that is what built the resilience in me in the first place. There are a lot more childhood stories I want to share. Stories that will give you an insight into the kind of person that I was and how I would turn out. So stick around, see you in the next chapter!

Chapter 3 - My Shenanigans...and Jack White's Nephews!

Where was I? Oh yeah, I was telling you about how I used to hide my brother's things before Christmas. I guess I was weird in that sense, but not without a cause. I had my reasons. There are two ways to look at it, and you can look at it this way: you can see that I loved my brothers so much I badly wanted to give those Christmas gifts and make them happy, you know? Anyhow, my shenanigans did not stop there. There was more. I was one of those kids, you know, the type who would sneak off with a Rubrics Cube and then complete it by removing all of the stickers and lining them correctly to show people I had done it. So, I had this cube that was all multicolored and pretty difficult to align. My solution was to take off one side and then replace it with all the red stickers. Then replace the next side with green. Ingenious, you could say? I was sick of trying to find the correct way and waste so much time trying to solve it, this was a shortcut, and you know how it goes; if it works, it works.

Then came pre-school. It was an immense pain for my parents, I think. I was a peculiar child, you could say. So it was difficult for my parents to find a pre-school for me. I had this idea that I was a big boy. You know, the one who did not need to nap or do all the basic kids' stuff most children my age did. Of course, that idea did not go down well with these pre-school people who thought the students should always comply. How ridiculous is that? I mean, that age makes or breaks you, so it is essential to let a kid's uniqueness shine instead of molding him into what you want him to be – like every other child that age. Eventually, I ended up in some church type pre-school. Go figure! It was weird, as many of us kids were put in some church basement, being preached Catholicism though I barely knew what all of it was at the time. The lady was nice, though. She told us to call her Mrs. Christ. It was funny if you ask me, but I guess that was her name, no matter how ironic. Thankfully though, this place did not really call for naps. There were seven of us in that pre-school, but all of them had dropped out by the end of the year. All of them except for me, anyway. When it was just Mrs. Christ and myself, she told me to call her grandma and brought me home once. It was weird, but she was a sweet woman. She introduced me to Chip, her son. I loved her. The best part was she was okay with me not taking naps, so for me, that was a big win.

At the time, my family lived in Detroit, which is now called East English Village. Maybe some of you live there right now or have probably heard of it. If you live there right now or have at some point, you would know that it has changed plenty. When I was there, it was a large square of streets, and the borders were Cadieux Road, East Warren, East Outer Drive, and Mack Avenue. Here is the thing though, if you were born on one side of Mack Avenue in Grosse Pointe, the chances are that you had a pretty good life. Your family was relatively wealthy. If you were born on the other side, in Detroit, you might have to struggle. That was the wealth disparity that existed at the time and probably still does. One invisible boundary separates the working class from the wealthy ones. You know, it reminds me of that phrase 'the other side of the tracks.' When you were born in Detroit, you had to work harder than anyone else. We lived on Kensington Street, and I am glad to say that we had this strong sense of a community bond. The strangers did not feel like strangers; it was more of a family bond. The kind of authentic family bond most of us try to have today. So, we were a pretty close-knit community, and I'm really proud of that.

The thing about close-knit communities is that when you know each other, you have fun together, and lots of it. We would have block parties where everyone would bring potluck. They were planned for months; Firefighters used to come and park their fire truck, and then the fire hose would squirt water on us kids. It was pretty good. Since we knew every person on the block, we would knock on their door and ask for candy whenever we wanted. Actually, to be fair, I would do that, and people were friendly enough to give me candy. Ms. Tanoose, an elderly lady that lived just to the right of us, was always happy to comply, but she did not have good candy. So I went to Max's house across the street and asked for candy because I knew they had Reese's peanut butter cups.

Fast-forward to 1984. I was a preschooler. I also had a wedding. Well, many neighborhood kids and my brothers decided to throw our wedding. It was a bit stupid because Ann Marie and I were more like brother and sister. But we went along with the show anyway because we thought, what's the harm? Plus, we were all having fun. It was a proper wedding; you know, the kind where people throw rose petals at you. There was Donkey Kong music playing out of an Atari 2600, and we even exchanged rings. It was funny, and I would say more romantic than some of the dates I had as a young adult.

Hillary from down the street and I were good friends. We spent a lot of time together as kids. She was a year older than me, and we used to play doctor every chance we got. I had no idea what the fascination was. Perhaps it was instinct, and I was growing up and exploring myself and my body. I would get her naked a lot of the time, and I remember there was a lot of kissing. We played doctor in this attic space attached to her bedroom in her house, and nobody would come to check on us. Other times, we would fool around on the side of my family's house in between Mrs. Tanoose's place and ours. I don't exactly remember when the doctor game turned into casual fooling around, but I remember that I had fun. Good times, considering.

This was a good year for me. We got a VCR, and I watched so many movies on it. 'The Karate Kid' and 'Beverly Hills Cop' were my absolute favorites. I also watched 'The Terminator,' 'Purple Rain,' 'Starman,' and who can overlook 'Indiana Jones'? One movie, in particular, stands out. It was 'A Christmas Story.' I remember watching it and thinking just how old it was. It's a bit funny, though. Because the thing is, it came out the year prior. I remember watching 'A Nightmare on Elm Street.' Man, that movie scarred me for life; I am still traumatized by it. Nothing gives me chills as that movie does. Folks, I am telling you. They don't make movies like that anymore.

I remember this one time my mom drove us to a drive-in movie theater to see a double feature of 'ET' and 'Gremlins.' On the way to the theater, I fell asleep in the backseat. I remember waking up and noticing that we were still not there. So I asked my brother how long until we get there, and everyone started laughing. It turns out they had already seen the movies and were on their way back home. I was so humiliated by this. You know, as I write this, I still don't understand why it is that my family did not wake me up. It's their idea of a joke, I presume. I did end up seeing 'ET' a little later in life. No wonder I hate it. Man, families can be so mean sometimes. I was looking forward to watching that movie in the theatre so much.

I then rolled Kindergarten. I felt I was ready, and I had what it takes to get there. I was tired of watching my big brothers go to big schools. Now, my time was finally here. I don't know what my fascination with being and acting older than my age was; sure, I was different from kids my age, but I think they need to act grown up from watching my older brothers. Anyhow, I was enrolled in St. Clare of Montefalco, where they split the class with an AM and PM class. Go figure. I had the AM class, and my mother walked me to school. I started to cry when we got there. I did not see this coming. I wanted my mother with me. Apparently, I created quite the fuss, man. I cannot believe it. For someone who wanted to be a big boy so bad, I sure did cling to my mom on the first day of school, Embarrassing. But I am glad to know that I settled down as soon as I walked into class.

I think I had one of the best teachers. Her name was Mrs. Blough, and she was so comforting. For show and tell, I would show the class my finger-painting skills. We even had this playroom, which had a toy kitchen. There were pots and pans lined up, and Jacklyn Joyce and I played house. I am sure she was like my wife there. After the class, I would go to daycare. Ray and his wife ran it. My parents were working full time, so going home directly was not an option. I went there and interacted with their children, Tony and Suzette, and other kids at the daycare. They would feed us, but I hated being fed peas. I told him no peas a couple of times, but Ray told me to just eat around them. Man, I was assertive even then. No naps, no peas, and I was adamant. You can see I have not really changed much. The punishment was minimum, thank God. We got to face the wall for 5-15 minutes if we were naughty. I got it a couple of times. I mean, what else can you really expect from me?

Despite my parents working full time, they still managed to take time out for us. We weren't that sad old cliché of working parents that neglected their children; after Kindergarten and daycare, we had more. One particular memory that stands out to me is from Oct 1984, when the Detroit Tigers had just won the World Series in baseball. My brothers and one of Scott's friends all got into the car and celebrated the big win. It was huge for us and called for a massive celebration. My father was the one who took all of us out, and we screamed our heads off the whole time. I had screamed so much that I ended up with laryngitis. Good times, though. My father loved baseball, as you can tell. And he loved me, in his own way at least. He was always pushing me to make new friends. I remember one Halloween; he pushed me to talk to this girl across the street, Chloe. I was just so embarrassed because my mother had talked me into dressing up as Cindi Lauper for Halloween. I had borrowed Chloe's socks. I cannot tell you how embarrassed I was. I took off running into the backyard and jumped a fence or two just to avoid talking to her.

I don't actually remember telling you what my parents did. My father worked full time on the assembly line at Chrysler and then went to night school at Wayne State University. He was there for eight years before he finally managed to graduate, and I admired that. He wanted to finish his education no matter what. He was determined enough to do it while simultaneously juggling a job and supporting his family. I remember the night of his graduation. It was such a party. People were pouring into our house, and it was overflowing at one point. I became a waiter, and I distributed the drinks. I served beer to anyone who wanted it. I think that was my first keg party. It was pretty awesome.

My mother worked for the City of Detroit, and they had a residency law requirement. If you were a city employee, you had to live there. The logic was that there were policemen and firemen around to protect you from crime. That was what they thought. That is one of the reasons why we lived there. My mother had started out as a teacher because that was her father's dying wish for her. For a couple of years, she did that and then returned to college to get a degree in Business Administration from Central Michigan University. So, both of my parents were extremely hard-working, motivated, and clear-headed.

My mother had her own quirks. She had a bizarre way of disciplining us. Enter Patricia, the new babysitter. Oh, how I missed Patty then. My mom wanted a stronger woman, you know, the kind who would keep the boys in check while she wasn't around. I can't blame her; a house full of growing boys is most people's nightmare. But not Patricia. Apparently, Patricia was that strong presence my mom wanted. She reminded me of that woman who was like Nanny 911, and you know that television show where they brought in this nanny to discipline the kids. My mother told her she should make us write essays if we broke a rule.

I felt that was the stupidest thing. I mean, of all punishments, why this? But it worked. I think mostly because I was this naïve child who believed Patricia every time she yelled, "If you don't come back to the house you will be grounded for the rest of your life." I can actually kick myself right now for believing this stuff. But I was five years old, what can you expect, right? I used to come back to the house and write the lines until my fingers hurt. They were pretty stupid lines like, "I will not talk back to my babysitter." While most people say this punishment's purpose was to reinforce rules by making us write them and internalize them, I would argue the punishment wasn't that. Nor the pain in my wrists after finishing those lines. The real punishment was how painfully boring it was to keep writing the same thing over and over again, and eventually, I had started listening to her just to avoid the lines.

All three of us hated her. This was one thing that my brothers and I could agree on. She was one of the worst babysitters, if not the absolute worst. I mean, she had to be on the list at least. My mother loved her for some reason. She thought we needed a hard one. I don't recall how she left, but she left, thank God! She made me miss Patty so much.

First grade arrived, and I remember it was pretty tough because we had this new teacher, Mrs. Wisniewski. She was super mean. I mean, I understand that teachers have to maintain discipline and teach us stuff outside the classroom, but she would downright bully certain kids and make them cry. She would definitely be on the list of traumas for those kids. Plus, Mrs. Blough was so nice and sweet to us. So this sudden shift really took us by surprise. It was a significant change. I think she was a sadist, which would explain why she was so unnecessarily cruel to kids. I remember she used to call Ryan Riley a big boob. She would pick up his desk and dump all of its contents on the floor. She berated him endlessly and had him straighten out his desk while the whole class watched. She was a horrible human being, I think. I don't know how such people could be allowed to be teachers. I mean, you are putting the minds of fragile children in the hands of complete strangers who could turn out to be so sadistic and traumatize them forever. It still baffles me how she became a teacher. Anyhow, my first-grade experience was saved when I met Hank. He became my best friend. I think that was the only good thing that came out of this. I also made friends with Big Dan. He was larger than everyone else, hence the nickname.

Hank was weird. He lived about two miles away, so he was not my neighborhood friend. My parents also did not want me going over to his house very often; I never fully understood why. Maybe because it was so far away, but probably not. This one time, Hank invited me to celebrate a Greek Orthodox holiday with his family. Finally, my father let me go to his place, but he freaked out as he drove me there. When he dropped me off, he told me that he did not like the area. I was, under no circumstances, allowed to leave the house. Maybe it was my father's words that lit a spark inside me to create trouble, or perhaps I just attract trouble without wanting to.

So, there we were at his house, having a blast. I suggested we have a pillow fight. Hank had a younger brother, Reggie, and I decided it would be a bit of fun to have a pillow fight with him. It's what my brothers and I did at home, so I really saw no harm. Plus, it was nice to finally have someone younger than me play pillow fight with me. My brothers were ruthless; they never really held back. It was always fun, though, so it makes sense how I saw no harm in it. But here is the thing, I rarely ever see the harm in anything. We switched off the light and began, and boy, oh boy, one of us pulled Reggie off the bed, and he lost his balance. He hit his head and the eye…got a black eye. He went crying to his mother, and I felt horrible. I felt like I was about to be kicked out. This was all my fault, and I had felt like I spoiled the family dinner. It was embarrassing and made me feel terribly guilty. I was a knucklehead.

Hank was not the brightest crayon in the box, though. I guess it was partly because of the background he came from. His mom, Daad, was Syrian and did not know a lot of English. His father, Reginald, was a tall Englishman, and they did not seem to get along. But then again, I was a kid. Who was I to judge what was happening or even read the situation correctly, but things did seem off. All I knew was that the dude was incredibly racist. Reginald did not want to move out of the house because his father had died there. So, even after the neighborhood turned into a living hell, he refused to move. Talk about wacky and toxic attachments. He lived on Manistique, google map it. It looks like a war zone. I remember it was Martin Luther King Jr.'s birthday in 1985. I was in school, and Hank was not there. I was wondering where he was. In the afternoon, he called my house and asked to speak to me. My parents were home because they had a paid holiday, so my dad asked Hank why he was home. He said it was because it was King Luther's birthday. He thought that meant a day off from school. I am telling you, I was friends with a bunch of dumbnuts. That has to tell you something about myself, no? One thing is certain, though; it is always the dumbnuts you have the most fun with.

Another friend I had was Dan Minor. He was different from Hank, and my parents were okay with him. Actually, his family and mine were family friends. Dan's parents got married in Las Vegas, and my parents were witnesses. So I spent a lot of time with Dan. We spent so much of our time watching movies and doing different other things. I remember the first time we watched a movie together, and it was 'The Last Dragon.' It was in the basement of my house. We watched the movie and were so riled up that we had to try out many moves on each other. Justin being Justin, kicked Dan really hard. Dan fell into this laundry barrel the next thing we know, and we covered him with dirty clothes. He was crying a lot. His cries for help and constant sobbing didn't stop us. Instead, we were giggling to the point our stomachs hurt! Two lessons from that day: Dan knew how we played in the house, and second, my brothers and I have an unusual concept of what fun is.

My shenanigans continued. By 1987, I was now in the second grade. I enjoyed it so much more than the first grade. I think it had a lot to do with the fact that I had a better teacher, Mrs. Lucas. She was so pretty; I think I had a crush on her. There was also another girl in my class, Emily. And you guessed it. I had a crush on her too. She made my heart flutter. She flashed us her underwear a couple of times, so that is probably why she made me have butterflies in my stomach. I think she knew the effects she had on us. So she used to lift up her skirt and twirl in her underwear. It was oddly lovely to look at, although I do wonder where she got this idea from. Flashing your underwear to a bunch of kids at school is not a normal thing to do. Regardless, I was so smitten. I even joined the choir just to be near her. I think men really do stupid things when they are around the people they love. Or when they fall in love. I was so tone-deaf when it came to singing. All I cared about was impressing her. This will be a repeated trait, as you will soon discover.

In the second grade, all of us would sit on the floor and watch 'Reading Rainbow.' I don't know if you guys know about this show. It was this television show about books, and it starred Lamar Burton. If you don't, just

Google it. During this time, Emily would play footsies with this boy Corey. When she did that, it would boil my blood; maybe that was the first time I felt jealousy. But since Corey and I were friends, I was okay with it. I wanted to be the one she could play footsies with. That never happened with us.

It was also around this time that my father started to coach me at soccer. I was ecstatic. I had played in Kindergarten, but my dad told me I played like I was out there chasing butterflies. I was not keeping my head in the game, and that always stuck with me. I was over the moon to have my dad as my coach, even though he was a bit harder on me than other people. I appreciated it all the same. I knew he had a heavy schedule with the job and the university studies. It was also our father-son bonding time. So I appreciated it even more. I did tell you my parents took out time for us, didn't I?

By the third grade, Emily had moved away, and I had a lousy teacher. Her name was Sister Colleen, and she was so mean. If I thought my first-grade teacher was terrible, this one was even worse. I firmly believe, even to this day, this woman had absolutely no business being around younger kids. My friend Corey once slapped Sister Colleen in the face. She had this handprint on her cheek, and he reacted immediately afterward. He panicked and ran home. His house was not next door either. It was a good eight blocks away, but he just ran, so you can imagine how scared he was. Everyone was shocked. It is sporadic to have complete silence in a room full of third-graders, but no one was even breathing then. Everyone was so stunned. Things like this did not happen in a Catholic school; ask anyone. I don't remember how it ended, but I do remember wondering what will happen next.

Since Emily went away, I had a new crush. This girl was Shavon, and she hated me. I was a bit sad. She didn't join the choir, and I was relieved. It worked out in my favor. Since she hated me, we never had anything to do with each other. I don't know why she hated me, though. Maybe she thought I was a trouble maker who was going to ruin things for her. She was half-right, though. I was a trouble maker. But then, all kids are. I crushed hard on Shavon all through grade school without even talking to her, but I learned to move on as I got older.

I was also part of the Cub Scouts, and we had this competition within our pack that took place annually. Pinewood derby cars are small wooden models that the Cub Scouts make with their families' help, just in case you are wondering. They race their cars, which are powered by gravity, down this track. You are given this pinewood block and make a sculpture out of it, with your parents' help. It should be within the weight limit set by the judges. If it is above, well, you are out of the competition. My father and I worked on this together; he kept coating the car with clear varnish, and the thing was, we did not have a scale to weigh it on, to see how we were doing. He just kept putting on the varnish. I think he managed to put on ten coats. Anyway, the day arrived, and when it came for my car to race, they put it on the scale. It was way over the limit. And I mean really over the limit. Luckily though, they used a machine to drill some holes into the derby car to bring down the weight. They kept carving and carving, and eventually, it didn't really pay off. It got to the point where they could not cut out any more wood. I had to be disqualified. I was sad, but at least my father was spending time with me. I was so happy about that. But I do wish he had not put on so much varnish. Ten coats, dad? Really?

I think I told you about Gilbert. He was my mother's brother. He was chosen to be my godfather as a peace offering. He and my mother were not on the best terms. Actually, they were barely getting along. Things were not really improving. Despite the peace-offering, it seems things would never get better. He did grace us with his presence. He would come on my birthday, bring a $15 toy and then drink $30 worth of liquor. He and his wife were extraordinary drinkers. A normal person brings one case of beer to share with his friends. Just between him and his wife, Carolyn, the two finished a case of beer. In fact, they did not go to the drive-in movies unless they had two cases of beer and maybe a fifth of liquor.

He also would not help with my grandmother, his own mother. Talk about being callous. He worked at Chrysler, and he was high up in the union. It was because of his father, and it is not as if he got there on merit. My grandmother was so sick and had lived in a condominium. My mother used to help her with rent and expenses, but he didn't offer much. I was so ashamed of having him as a godfather. I am so grateful that it stayed just a title, and he never had the chance to play the role. Justin, my brother, had the best godparents. They were Sue and George, and my mother knew them from high school. Sue worked at Kmart with executives. Things worked out in Justin's favor, always. She managed to get him these Nintendo games before they were even released to the public. They were the newest kind, and I was a bit jealous. Here, my brother was getting the most amazing and unique gifts from his godparents, and I had godparents who could not even be bothered to spend on family. There came a time when my mother stopped talking to Gilbert altogether, and if my brothers had shared their stuff with me, I would not really have cared that much. But they did not.

Justin had middle child syndrome, and he demanded so much attention from my parents. You have no idea. Because of this, he got so much more attention from our parents. Sometimes it was as if Scott and I did not exist. He was the one who got the video games, and he was always so mean to me. You know one of those people who would come in and reset the game no matter what level I was playing on. It happened to me so many times on so many different levels that I have actually lost count. He was also the kind who would throw tantrums. We had an Intellivision game system in the early 80s, and I can't tell you how many controllers he broke from throwing them at the TV. He made life so difficult. He would taunt me mercilessly, but there was one advantage in this. I ended up growing a very thick skin like the kind where I just do not care at all. Justin, if you're reading this, sorry for spilling out your secrets. I would like to point out that things have greatly improved between us in recent years. The past is behind us. I guess in some way, all of us were a handful.

My grandparents were pretty awesome people, especially my grandpa. We would spend a lot of time there. And I mean, a lot. We would go over there as a family for dinner and end up staying a few hours. I think we were there every other week or so, at least that is what it felt like. One has a weird sense of time when one is younger. My grandpa had this Crown Royal Bag, and he would keep his pennies in there. He gave them to me whenever I came over. I used to wait to go over there just for this. It made me feel so important to touch that bag. Plus, my grandpa worked at a bank, so he would give us these cool checkbooks that were full of dollar bills at Christmas time. I felt like a grown-up. I used to peel out the dollars like they were checks and spend them. Those were good times.

Then, we moved. My parents had been contemplating doing this for a long time. They either wanted to move to Arizona or San Diego, California. It was because of this that we put our Kensington house for sale. It was a sad moment. I would miss this house, but I was also excited. See, we were moving to this place on Bishop Street. This was about three blocks away from where I had currently lived, and I had all my friends there. Stephen and Benjamin lived there, and so did Big Dan. Corey lived a few doors down too.

Okay, so I told you earlier that I will talk about Jack White. I don't know if you guys know him or not. He is an American musician, and his real name is John Gillis. He is known all around the world as a fantastic musician.

Not that I am advertising his work or anything. I knew him before he became Jack White. So here is the story. When we moved onto Bishop Street, I met Benjamin and Stephen. They were both nephews of Jack White. He also had a niece named Angela, who was their sister. Stephen was my age, and Benjamin was a couple of years younger. But you know, I started to hang out with Benjamin. I was not really hanging around Stephen until the 4th grade. As we would call him, Benjamin or BJ was a bit weird, but then I think, you know by now just how wacko my friends were. He used to walk around in these long shirts and pants, even in the sweltering heat during the summer, the ones that had camouflage print. He wanted to join the military, and he was doing whatever he could to live up to the role, I think. GI Joe was all the rage at the time, and it's all we played with. BJ thought joining the military was going to be like an episode of GI Joe.

Then, as time went on, I started to hang out around Stephen. We were still friends all the way through high school and beyond. He had this desire to become an actor. I don't think it went well for him, but he's still trying. We were both these huge Steven Spielberg fans and asked him if we could be in one of his upcoming movies. We had seen 'Goonies' at the time, and we got so excited. We were running around thinking this was going to be our big break. Little kids, eh? We were really disappointed when Steven's secretary sent a form letter. We continued to work on our material, though.

I wanted to become a filmmaker or an actor. So Stephen and I made a nice pair. We were writing our own scripts and stories in the 3rd and 4th grades, as I said. He had this habit of walking around the parking lot scribbling something in his notebook, but he never showed what it was. Said it was a play, and that is that. He said he would only give you a part if he liked you. I had a few original ideas, too, which I did not show off either. I guess we were hesitant. It is challenging to put yourself out there. I am sure different artists would agree.

We also had subscriptions to Entertainment Weekly, and it was a pretty good publication at that point. With the advent of the internet, I think it ceased to exist, maybe not. We loved the movies at the time. They were so not like the ones today. Have you seen the re-boot version of 'Ghostbusters'? They replaced all the men with women. Why? What was the point? The special effects are good, but the plot is just horrible. Yet, they make profits. I wonder how. I guess the younger generation has a different taste.

Around this time, John Gillis, also known as Uncle John to us, visited us at Stephen's house on Bishop Street. He came from a huge family, and he was not really that much older than Stephen and me. He was the brother of my friend's mother. It is a bit weird though, imagine having an uncle who is almost the same age as you. Their family was pretty big, from what I have heard. I think they were ten siblings in all, and he was the youngest one. He came to babysit Stephen, BJ, and Angela, and I would usually be there with them. He was a nice fellow, though. I remember when 'Back to the Future 3' came out. They were playing the trilogy of the three movies at this one theater far away from our house. We begged Stephen's mother to take us. Erik, another friend from our school, also participated in this charade. So Stephen's mother dropped us off at his grandparents and Uncle John's house while we waited for one of Stephen's other uncles, the baker, to pick us up and take us to the movie trilogy. The three of us were snooping around Uncle John's bedroom; I remember that.

But I don't really have a lot of memory regarding what we found. For the sake of this book, I wish I would have taken a better mental inventory of what we discovered. I do remember the trilogy was sold out and we went all the way out there for nothing. We saw another movie instead. I'm sure Stephen remembers what it was too.

My story doesn't end here. My shenanigans continue my entire life, basically. So sit back, enjoy the ride and

watch what comes up. Who knows, you might find my life
as entertaining as I do.

Chapter 4 – Back When I Wasn't Nostalgic

In 1988, my parents moved to San Diego, California. They wanted to stay near my dad's sister, Janice. Therefore they chose Spring Valley to settle. My parents rented a Ryder truck, and we filled it up with our belongings. Their friend John had agreed to drive the moving truck for us, so my parents could save some money. We went on the journey in two cars, and it took us five days to get to California. We arrived at my aunt's empty house on Thanksgiving Day. They had made plans for Thanksgiving dinner elsewhere. I noticed my cousin Don had a slingshot in his bedroom. When I saw that, I immediately wanted one. Of course, getting one would not be that easy. Whether my parents could afford it or not was never a problem I worried about. They would either tell me that it was too expensive or worthless to buy or that they would get something better from somewhere else, which never happened. It was always quite the effort to convince my parents that this is what would complete my life. It was just a slingshot, but nothing else was on my mind. I pestered my parents over the next few weeks, and they only agreed with the condition that both my and Justin were careful with them. Once we agreed, they finally bought one each for the both of us.

The very next day, we were both quite excited to try out our slingshots at the mountain trail. Justin and I grabbed our slingshots and headed off to a mountainous terrain that was right next to our house. On our way there, I envisioned myself having a sort of epic skirmish with Justin, as we would hide behind a big boulder shooting each other with rocks. Once I got there, I decided to give it a little test run first. I picked up a rock, placed it in the leather strap, pulled the elastic back as far as it would go and released it. Justin was standing close to me, and the rock hit him directly behind the ear. I'm surprised he didn't drop to the ground. He ran to the house. He could have died. I was remorseful, but he thought I did it on purpose, which I did not. He was sore but was otherwise fine. Our parents took our slingshots away the first day we had them. Such was my life. Oh well.

Then the time came around for Middle School. I was a Highland Hooter at Highland Middle school, and I was a fresh student in the 4th grade. Highland was absolutely crazy when you would compare it to St. Clare's private school, which was essentially its polar opposite. There was hardly any order in the school. Mr. Velenta was my new 4th grade teacher. I had a classmate named Tyson, and Mr. Velenta just put him in the back of the room where he would continue to disrupt the class. He knew how to rile up the kids in the class. I thought he was cool, and I liked his name as well, and I thought he was funny. He was a popular kid in the school.

The hallways of the school were outdoors, which was strange to me. On my very first day there, I got picked on by some kids briefly because I had a very noticeable lisp, you know, like Mike Tyson. After the initial burns wore off, I put my big boy pants on and played with them. A kid named Chris asked if I liked the Lions, and I said, "Not this season. They *thuck*." Luckily, instead of Chris picking on me, we both had a good laugh about it all. Months later, I would dig through Chris' father's porn stash with him. He still had an Intellivision set, which was unheard of. Intellivision was a game console that came out around the same time as Atari. I had a ton of games left that were unused because our console was broken, so I sold them to him. Chris became a good friend.

Once I saw Aimee on the playground she became my crush immediately. She was a pretty little blonde girl with blue eyes. I would try to get close to her so I could steal some of her glimpses. I did not know anybody yet and had not made friends, so that is what I did for recess. After spending a couple of weeks at school, I found out that Aimee was dating Tyson and that he was the most popular kid at school. Somehow, I got snaked into dating her friend Amanda instead of Aimee. I got my very own first cassette tape that year. It was *Forever Your Girl* by Paula Abdul in 1988. I wore out that tape too!

I started really liking Amanda, to my surprise. I liked Aimee more, but I was not too picky. By dating, I mean that I went to her house two or three times and talked to her on the phone a few times. I was in 4th grade, there isn't much we know enough about to do it at that age, so it wasn't really an issue. Of course, I remembered what I did with Hillary and wanted to do it with Amanda too. Then a strange thing happened. After a few weeks, Amanda broke up with me, saying that the only reason she had dated me was to figure out if I was a good fit to date Aimee. That was a punch in the face to me. Amanda was the first girl who made me cry over a break-up. I cried well and hard. A question started spinning across my mind: well, Amanda, am I a good enough fit to date Aimee? I am still waiting for the answer. Perhaps she simply forgot, or maybe she lost my number and could not call me anymore. Yes, that might be it. I bet she would call any day now. Regardless, I could not bear to hear the Paula Abdul cassette after that.

There were other things in my life besides being taken for a test drive by girls. My aunt, uncle, and cousins lived down the street. Things were great in my world. My father struggled for a while to find a decent job but eventually landed one with a living wage, and things appeared to be good. My mom had got a job before we had moved, so we had some disposable income. As for my friends, I met Jimmy, who lived across the street and down the way a little. He was my first friend in California, and he was cool. We would go to each other's house almost every day and would hang out for hours. If anyone would ask where I was, my parent's first thought was that I would probably be at Jimmy's. We played a lot of basketball and video games while we were in grade four. I also made a friend Jesse who told me that his father was a stunt man for Kevin Costner. I found it really cool. I never saw him, nor did it change my opinion of Kevin Costner.

It was during that time when my dad's brother, Tom, moved in with my Aunt Janice and Uncle Pete down the street from the house we were renting. It was great to catch up with him because I had only seen him occasionally while growing up. There was a community park that our family would go to and play basketball. It was Scott, Justin, Uncle Pete, Uncle Tom, Cousin Donovan, and me. I was ten years old, and there was one shot that I rarely missed, and that was from the free-throw line. They started calling it my "old faithful" shot. I would always stand up there and wait for the ball. We played a lot of basketball. Afterward, we would go to the 7-11 for a big gulp. I remember I used to watch the droplets seep through the cold cup and onto the table. It fascinated me.

Uncle Tom worked in the construction field, and one day while on top of a two-story building, a crane bumped into him while he was looking in the other direction. He fell from 2 stories and landed on his two heels and hip. He shattered his heels and broke his hip, and was laid up for a long time at the house of Aunt Janice and Uncle Pete. They brought in a hospital bed, and he was laid out in the family room for quite a few months. He was never the same after that accident. He only received $50,000 in a settlement case. Was that enough to last for the rest of his life? I thought not. It was not even enough for him to start his life over, now that walking would become a near-impossible aspiration of his.

In the summer, my mother's best friend Libby and her two boys, Scott and Jamie, arrived in California from Detroit for a visit. Scott was of the same age as my brother Scott, and Justin was of the same age as Jamie. While they were there, we went to Universal Studios Hollywood. I was ten at the time and super excited for the experience. We could see the A-Team van, which was important to me because Justin and I used to take big old cardboard boxes like a refrigerator box and make the A-Team van out of them. We used pens or markers to add buttons and other stuff. We also saw the KIT car that Michael Knight drove in Knight Rider. I was most excited about seeing the clock tower from Back to the Future. They had a ride called "Earthquake" that reflected what would happen in a subway station during an earthquake. That was huge, and it was a fun experience.

When we were driving through LA, Libby and my mother played a trick on Scott. Both my brother Scott and his friend Scott had huge crushes on Alyssa Milano. Libby pointed out a random house and told him it was hers, saying how she purposely didn't live in luxury to avoid others but that she and Milano were good friends. Scott, being somewhat impressionable when it came to his celebrity crush, believed her and went to the door asking for Alyssa as if she was expecting him. Some bewildered person answered the door, confused, before looking in the direction of our car and realizing what was happening. Scott came back to the car feeling like an ass. That is how our mothers acted. They were dying with laughter. Parents always have the most fun at the expense of their children, don't they?

We also went to the original Hard Rock Cafe in Hollywood, which meant something special for us. That was the restaurant that started with a $10 burger. In 1988, the price was a lot. Perhaps Hard Rock's burgers are selling for $20 now, or perhaps they have closed down because fast food should not be that expensive. I do not know because I do not go there anymore. Detroit was the last major city, probably in the world, to get a Hard Rock Cafe.

Justin's birthday came around, and he received a basketball hoop for his special day. It was called the Harvard mini court, and you could roll it into the garage or move it around and place it where you wanted. When we played basketball, it was always Scott and me on a team and Justin and Donovan on the other team. The oldest with the youngest made sense to us. There was so much smack talking, fighting, and crying on the court that we still talk about it. Justin would get upset almost every time we played. He would grab the basketball hoop and start rolling it away and into the garage. If he was upset, nobody could play. It is sort of a privilege that we had among us friends. If you had a game console everyone played on, who got to play it was your decision.

Justin was in a baseball league that was all serious and competitive, and the diamonds were maintained very well. They used the major-league teams, and he was on the Philadelphia Phillies. The league was for kids aged 12-13, and Justin was 13. Tyson, from my 4th grade class, was also in the league because he was older and was held back. I remember the family going to Justin's games to cheer him on. He was a pitcher, and during one game, he beaned a kid in the face and broke his nose. I don't remember how well a pitcher he was. Just that he beaned some kid at the plate and was in tears from remorse afterwards.

My parents and Libby took Justin and me to Tijuana, Mexico, for a day. It's right on the border of Mexico and California and is known as a shit hole. My dad told us to watch out for ourselves. He said that they liked blonde-haired kids, and someone might snatch us. That scared the shit out of me. I still do not know whether he was being serious. Later on, I would find that being snatched as a blonde kid was the least of my concerns. While we were there, my mother found a guy selling cassette tapes on the street. After we had all picked a few out, she started haggling with the guy to where she told us to put our tapes back. We were bummed out, but my mother assured us he would come back around, and we could get the tapes for even cheaper and better quality to boot. He never came back. However, Libby bought a sombrero for each of us.

On the way back to California, our car had a flat fire, and we were stuck on the side of the road in Tijuana. It was a Sunday night, so all the shops were closed. It was actually the second spare that had been shredded, which showed that we were out of luck. Luckily, a taxicab pulled over in front of our parked car and asked us if he could be of any help to us. My father took a ride with the guy and left the four of us in the car on the side of the road. Of course, being left alone by my father in Tijuana, with my mother being obviously scared as well, made me feel abandoned. She says now that she was worried if my father would ever come back, but she kept that to herself. After waiting for an hour, but what seemed much longer than that, a taxi pulled back up in front of our car, and out came my dad. He had a tire with him, too, so now all we had to do was put the tire on and be on our way. Justin and I looked like idiots with our sombreros on, just standing there helplessly watching our father do all the work.

We were still a wrestling family, so Scott and my cousin Donovan would make a tag team to wrestle against Justin and me. They called themselves Capitol Punishment, and they named us the Sombrero Brothers. I had a black sombrero and Justin had a blue one. It was not anywhere near fair because they were bigger than both of us and could easily take us down. To top it all off, they even made a couple of championship belts out of cardboard and tin foil. They would wave them around as if they were a big deal or something. They were just a couple of bullies. Justin and I would always try to get our hands on those belts, but they kept them hidden at my cousin's house out of our reach. It would have been nice to wave them in their face for once. In age, Donovan was in between Scott and Justin. I was 10, Justin was 13, Donovan was 15, and Scott was 16.

I had another cousin, Donovan's sister, Stacey. She's a year older than Scott, so while I was 10 years old, she was 17. We didn't spend a lot of time together, because she was doing her teenaged things and I was doing my kid stuff, but she was always really nice when we came to their house. When the movie Child's Play with Chucky came out, she took my brothers and me to the movies to see it. Stacey's really pretty and did some modeling back at the time. She gave me a pin to wear with her picture on it and I sported it like a pro. I would wear it on my jean jacket and when people would ask me who it was, I'd proudly say, 'that's my cousin'.

In the 5th grade, I had just settled into school and had a couple of friends, Chris and Jimmy. I had started the new grade with more confidence. I had friends to joke with that can make a world of a difference. Shortly after, I had settled in the school, my mother developed breast cancer at age 40. It was a tough decision to make whether to go back to Michigan, so we can be around our grandparents if the situation goes south, or to stay in California. She was given a 50/50 chance of survival. My mother had kept her illness from my brother, Justin and me. Scott was 16, so I'm sure he knew what was going on. She just didn't want us to know, because she didn't want us to worry about her. My parents moved back to Michigan after living less than a year in California.

We started packing up the house, loading up the truck, and saying goodbye to my Aunt Jan, Uncle Pete, Uncle Tom, and my cousins Stacey and Donavan. We had to make that miserable five-day trip across the country again. Sometimes, I would get car sick during these trips, and I found that you always seem to have to pee in these trips.

Luckily, there were plenty of stops, partly because of me and Justin. Well, mostly because of me. This time Scott went back to Detroit early, so he would not miss too much high school. Therefore, Justin and I had our own backseat in each car for the ride back. Little things matter on long trips. My mother let me drive for a few miles on the empty freeway. That was pretty kick ass. Luckily, I was old enough not to have to sit on someone's lap. It was nothing but open road for this 10-year-old.

When we returned to Detroit, we rented a house on Harvard Street until my parents could find a house to purchase. Now I lived on the same street as Dan Minor, one of my oldest friends. Dan lived about eight houses down from me. Ryan was another friend of mine that lived right across the street from Dan. They both had corner houses. Directly behind our house, there was a kid named Richard that we later nicknamed Rico. He was Justin's age, and they became good friends.

Ryan was a kid that I met hanging around the neighborhood. His father left him as a kid, and his mother, Sue, was dating a man named Thom. Even after his mother and Thom had broken up, Thom still treated Ryan as his own son, and would let him stay with him. He had an outstanding setup in his basement with a pool table and pin-ball machine. There was no supervision at the house, because Thom was gone all the time and perhaps he wanted to be the cool dad, or a fun uncle for the rest of us, whichever fit the bill. It would turn into the devil's playground for us in a few years.

The school year had already begun, and I was placed in Mrs. Heck's 5th grade class. It was nice to be back to where I had many friends and knew everyone. Mrs. Heck was a wacky lady, though. She would go on long tangents and storm around the room. I did not care for her, but she was nowhere near as bad as Mrs. Wisniewski in first grade and Sister Colleen in the third grade. She did remind me of them though, and I was thankful that they did not appear in my nightmares. Mrs. Heck, however, was a good person to laugh at. I know that we all must respect our teachers, but we were kids. Our moral compass was defined by who brought the ball or looked coolest.

I had tried out for and had made the basketball team at St. Clare, and we had a superb player on the team named Kenny. He stood out from anyone else and he could handle the ball, actually knew how to dribble properly, and was a good passer and shooter. We did not have the best season, but we had a good time. Most of the time on the court we would just look for Kenny to give the ball to, and the coach would always congratulate him for being the best among us, and how we should be more like him. I was a decent player and larger than a lot of kids my age, but nobody compared to him. He was, in every sense of the word, a natural.

Kyler came in as a new student in the 5th grade. His father was our basketball coach, and we became friends and played sports together. People in Detroit were getting robbed for their shoes around this time. We didn't have to worry about that though, because our parents would not buy us Air Jordans. I begged my dad for a nice pair of shoes for the basketball season that year. I wanted the $80 Reebok Pumps and my father said to me, "I don't even wear $80 shoes. What makes you think I'm going to buy them for you?" He ended up making it happen though, and I ended up getting the Pumps. I was grateful. I took superb care of them. They were the coolest pair of kicks I've ever had. When I pumped them up, it improved my game by 67%. Of course, it is not up to me to show any evidence of that statistic, but let me tell you. Just wearing that expensive pair made me feel better about myself, and I would just tear through the court. To my relief, my shoes were never stolen. They weren't Air Jordans, but that did not matter to the thugs in Detroit.

Stephen had a sleepover that year with a bunch of classmates over his house. It was Kyler, Jeff, Hank, Dave, a few others, and myself. The goal for the night was to sneak out of the house, because that is what we did during sleepovers. Stephen lived next door to a used car dealership, so that made it much more fun. When we would have sleepovers, we would usually buy a few cans of Jolt. It was soda that had a lot of caffeine in it, and we would use that to stay awake. The soda was not delicious, but it did the trick.

Bob Maxy's used car dealership was literally 30 feet away from Stephen and B.J.'s house on Bishop. There was a gated section of the dealership where they stored used cars that were not being displayed on the lot. We would sneak into the gated section by climbing up the fence, and we would check for cars that had unlocked doors. We discovered that the dealership would put the keys to other cars in the glovebox of another. We would grab the keys out of the glovebox and search for the other car that the keys went into. Once all of us had keys and found the cars that went with them, we would get into them. Then we would turn on the radio and start the car to turn on the air conditioner. There was nowhere to go because we were fenced in. But it was still exhilarating, pretending to drive and drift around in just about any car we chose.

My mother made it through chemotherapy and was given a good prognosis. Since she never told Justin and me in the first place, we had little idea of what was going on, which made it difficult for us to feel relieved. I just feel bad now that we know how bad we acted while she was going through such a hard time. She went through chemotherapy while still working and carried on as if nothing happened.

Ann Marie, my first bestie, and I thought it would be a good idea to date this year. I don't know what gave her that idea, but I did not care. I thought I'd make her a great romantic poem and she would fall head over heels. I gave her a ring and typed up a poem using a typewriter. We did not even kiss, and it only lasted a little while. I do not know what happened. We made better friends. It was kind of awkward, because until then I had viewed her as a sister. We were still cool afterwards, so at least it was not a messy break-up. I do think, though, that this experience taught me about how love and friendship works differently.

Dan Minor was a grade ahead of me, and we would walk to school together. I had a trusty pair of roller skates in the garage. Dan had an idea one day while we were running late for school. We each put one skate on and push off with our other foot. It was like pushing a skateboard, except it was just one roller skate that was strapped onto your foot. When we would get close to the school, we would find some bushes and stash the roller skates in there. Then we would grab them out of the bushes when school was finished and put them in our bag for the next day. We were not looking for attention either. We did not want to be seen by anybody while we were riding in the afternoon. It was for pure functionality, and we only did it when we were running late.

On one occasion, Dan had borrowed a sweater from his dad and wore it to my house for a sleepover. After getting into bed and falling asleep, Dan was awakened in the early morning. He woke up with my dog, Spencer, on top of his chest, chewing enormous holes into the sweater he was wearing. He was livid, and I was laughing my ass off. Dan said, "That's my dad's new shirt!" I just about died. I was laughing so hard.

By the time I had gotten into 6th grade; baseball was pretty much my life. I played basketball too, but I really liked baseball better, and mostly worked developing my baseball game, watching professional teams when I could so I could understand the game better, and practicing as much as I was able. The team at our school was for boys in the 6th, 7th, and 8th grade. Although I made the team as a sixth grader, I was always playing in the outfield or sitting on the bench. There was not much to do but watch being a substitute, and starting games was out of the question. As the sixth grader, I was always told to 'stay alert' for when they would need me, and to not say anything in the meantime. The coach would talk about how nothing is better than the real thing for getting match practice, though whenever I inquired about when I could play, he would just say something like, "watch and learn, you will get your chance soon kid." That continued for a while. I played outfield that year.

My parents found a house to buy on the next street over, named Cadieux. I was even closer to Dan and Ryan's house now. My parents paid $36,000 for the 3-bedroom house. There was a vast park behind our house, named Mesmer, and we had a gate in our backyard that led right to it. There was a baseball diamond where our school would play baseball. Some playground equipment like broken swings and a slide were at the opposite side of the baseball diamond. Justin and I had to share a bedroom, and Scott had his own right across the hall from us.

In the back of the garage, there was a little room that was probably meant for tools, but I made it to my clubhouse and set it up. It had its own entrance from the outside, and it had an entrance from the garage. We bought a large piece of plywood to cover the entrance in the garage. Therefore, it was a closed room. I built a table and a bed that was like a top bunk without its bottom half, because it was raised high off the ground. I found a carpet to lie down in there, and it became a place for us to hang out or just sleep when we would feel like it.

My maternal grandmother Jean came to live with us, because her health had deteriorated while in Florida and she needed care and attention. My parents bought a used hospital bed that could be raised, lowered, and moved into any position, and they put it in the dining room. Since there were only bathrooms in the basement and upstairs, we had to accommodate her with a commode, which is a portable toilet. I emptied that thing more times than I would like to remember, and it is not a memory I prefer recalling. I am sure you would understand why, so let us just move on from there.

Andrea was my neighbor on Cadieux and became my girlfriend around age 12. I could do all my kissing practice with her. I did not get to see her that often because it was her aunt's house on Cadieux and she lived with her mother, which was in between Seven and Eight Mile off of Kelly Road. It was pretty close to the Novara house that Eminem talks about in his music, so it had that going for it, however much good that did. My father dropped me off over her house and we would hang out for the day, and then I would call for a ride home. It became routine for a little while. When she was at her aunt's house. Once a week, I would invite her over to the clubhouse. Bow-chick-a-wow-wow. Later in life, I saw her on an episode of Hard Core Pawn.

Our entire grade went to a place called Camp Tamarack during the school year. Our grade compromised of two classrooms with 30 kids in each, so there were about 60 of us. Going to a camp was something that all students at St. Clare got to experience once they reached the 6th grade. It was a cool experience, because I was with my friends, and our teachers were much less strict with us. They almost seemed like genuine people. There were two boy's cabins and two girl's cabins in which we all stayed, and each one had a counselor. The highlight of the trip was that when a few of us, only guys, went near the women's restroom and took a glimpse of the tits of a fellow student Charlita. Once she saw us outside the window, she put on a show. Good times at Camp Tamarack. Sorry Charlita!

My school was on the Grosse Pointe side of Mack Avenue and my parents sent us there, because the public schools in Detroit were horrible. There was a place called the Grosse Pointe War Memorial that was on Jefferson, near Lake St. Clair on the Grosse Pointe side that held dances for students in 6th, 7th, and 8th grade Grosse Pointe students. If we wanted to attend the dances, we had to purchase an id card with our picture on it for $10 and then pay $5 to gain entrance to the dance.

Hank and I prepared for this dance by making a trip to Eastland Mall, which was on Eight Mile to find outfits. While looking for the outfits, Hank came across some black suede overall shorts. He suggested that each of us buy a pair and wear different undershirts. I got dressed up before the dance and borrowed a White Sox jersey from my brother Scott to wear with my suede overalls. Hank came by with a red shirt underneath and we got in my dad's car so he could take us to the dance. About halfway there my dad said to us, "Are you guys sure you don't want me to take you home for a change of clothes, just in case?" We were irritated with him, because we thought we looked fresh. We were idiots. At our age, it was evident that we had little to no fashion sense, or any general worry about our surroundings when it came to etiquette. We did not even use words like 'etiquette.' We were in preppy Grosse Pointe, where the kids were wearing polo shirts and khakis, and where they were always polite in front of the adults. Of course, my dad was right about the change of clothes. We stuck out like sore thumbs and were called Wiggers by a bunch of Grosse Pointe students. One guy told Hank he had better run. There was no physical confrontation, but we definitely learned our lessons and dressed like preppies for the next dance.

Our basketball team, as I've already mentioned, was coached by Kyler's dad. We had the all-star player named Kenny, and he was superb, often being the member of the team everyone relied on to be the match winner. The other guys on the team were my friends Brian, David, Mike T., and Mike. There was a kid named Julian that went to our school, and he was in the 8th grade. He was so good at basketball that our parents would come to watch us play just so they could stay for his game. Our team was decent, but Julian, who was like a Michael Jordan of the grade school overshadowed us.

Since Brian was in Grosse Pointe public schools and played sports with us and because he was part of our parish, he knew more about trending music and other cool stuff which we Catholic school kids did not. For instance, he introduced us to Nirvana when the Never Mind album came out and he got us into gangsta' rap, like Ice Cube's Amerikkka's Most Wanted. He showed us many things and he could answer my questions on drugs too. I remember asking him what 'pot' was. He informed me it was just another term for marijuana and weed. He was knowledgeable at that point in our lives, and we were not.

The parental advisory stickers had just recently come out and now you would have to be 18 to purchase hardcore music. Lucky for me, there was a boutique on E. Warren that sold all kinds of random things. Clothing mostly, but this one carried cassette tapes as well. They did not give a damn about selling us those cassettes. People would come there to buy rhinestones for their hats and clothing. Not me personally, but some people were decorating their hats with original color Rhine stones. That trend did not last very long. The second cassette that I owned was Ice Cubes' Amerikkka's most wanted, and we bought it from the boutique. I say 'we' because I only owned half of the tape and Dan owned the other half; we went halves on it.

During the summer, our baseball coach Pete took me and my friends to a Toledo Mud Hens baseball camp. The Mud Hens are the AAA team for the Detroit Tigers, so it's the last stop in the minor leagues before being called up to the Major League. Pete had organized for me, Mike T., and Mike to attend a baseball camp that was being held for a week. We stayed at the Hampton Inn on Reynold's Ave. in Toledo about a mile from the stadium, and every morning bright and early, we would drive down to the ballpark. Players from the Mud Hens would run drills with us and work with us one on one. They were good times. Getting to work on baseball at this level was exhilarating.

The summer after 8th grade, around 1993, is when I began drinking and smoking weed. My friends Ryan and

Dan had been smoking for a little while and kept wanting to get me high. I resisted for a long time and when they would smoke, I'd buy a couple 40 oz. beers and drink while they did their thing. Ryan had found a small stash in Thom's belongings and that's what Dan and Ryan were smoking. To secure the 40 oz., we would wait for a homeless person or college age kid and pay them to buy us beer.

Over that summer as I started to drink and smoke until the wee hours in the morning, is when I realized that my paper route days might as well be numbered. The newspaper was guaranteed to be delivered by 6 am and I was waking up around 9 or 10, hungover and still drunk. I'd bike it over to Yorkshire and get the papers delivered. I don't recall ever getting any bad feedback for being so late. Some days Morris, Stephen dad, would come to pick me up and they would bang on the door for a few minutes trying to wake me up. Sometimes they had to leave without me, which wasn't a huge deal. I just had to bike it instead of getting a ride. It sucks when you're hung over though and the Sunday papers were extra heavy with advertisements.

Ronnie was a neighbor of ours on Cadieux. He lived around six houses away from me. He was a friend of ours for the most part. We smoked with him a lot and he was, generally, a nice guy. He could be really shady though, too. I was driving home from my paper route and Ronnie stopped me on the corner and starts talking to me. As soon as he said, "You're bull shitten' with me," these two thugs came out of nowhere and they both punched me in the face at the same time. Ronnie had set me up. I was shocked, I didn't even know that it was two fists that hit my face at the same time until he told me later. They came out of nowhere and it all happened so quickly. I scratched him from my 'friends' list.

The metal bar that is on men's bicycles was broken in two after the jumping. I'm not really sure how that happened, because I had two fists in my face. I came home with my nose bleeding and my father asked me what had happened. He stormed out of the house with me on his tail and he jogged the six houses down Cadieux to Ronnie's house and confronted the three thugs. My father grabbed one of the kids, named Andrew, and started dragging him towards our front lawn.

My father wanted a fair fight, so he dragged Andrew to our front yard and told me to kick his ass. I regret to say, I did not want to fight even though I knew I could take him. The fact of the matter is I thought he had punched me himself and that punch knocked me on my ass and had broken my bike. Could this little runt really punch that hard?

It is only weeks later that Ronnie had told me it was two kids punching me at the exact same time. I chickened out of the revenge match, because I thought this fool punched like Mike Tyson!

We suspected Ronnie also broke into our house and stole Justin's video games and my grandmother's wedding ring, but we couldn't prove it. My grandma was living with us and her wedding ring came up missing, so we tore the house apart looking for it and then just concluded it was Ronnie. I have a lot of stories with Ronnie in them. He was a likable person if you could put the shadiness aside and watch your back. He was sentenced back in 2000 and was paroled in 2015. They had a lot of different charges on Ronnie. Assault with Intent to rob while armed with a minimum sentence of 13 years behind bars. He had 6 charges of menace against him. One for home invasion, possessing a felony firearms, and armed robbery. This guy was the Menace II Society in my area of Detroit.

I only wish the years in my life further down the line had all this naiveté and innocence. I was a hopeful kid, always trying to fit in, and sometimes succeeding, and getting in all sorts of mischief in the process. They were times of merrymaking and having fun at baseball camp. Later on, though, when I'd come well into my teenage years, a few hapless incidents would lead me to some equally unfortunate consequences.

Chapter 5 - Reminiscing, Partying and DUI's

Life can perhaps best be described as a blur, but a one that doesn't speed past us until we come to realize how fast and far away we have gotten. Every day seems to be a challenge, and we think that time just goes by ever so slowly until we come to realize that we have been living the same days over and over again. It hits like a train, waking us up to the fact that while we were wondering about living life, how time seems to go on forever, we missed the train altogether. The events just seem to blend together as a blur, and it's hard to distinguish between them. The days can start to gel together. You can try to think about it yourself. What did you do yesterday? The day before? It is how you forget what you ate for lunch or when you last went outside to get the groceries. You never really remember doing the laundry or washing the dishes, do you? Keep looking into the past, and soon you will dig deep into a place where all you can see is a blur. The blur continues into our everyday life as we repeat the same experiences and forget them. The blur fills in the blanks.

This is especially true when we are young. When we are young, we don't have to worry about the world around us. We can often just choose to ignore it and let it all blend into one memory. We don't always have to worry about finances or other things like that, and we can basically do what kids do. Our worries about tomorrow are not about how we live life, but just living it as it is, without thinking about a better tomorrow. Not having a past to relate to, at least early in life, is actually a blessing. You do not know that the good times have gone past you. As adults, we are always reminiscing about how the times have changed, and the times do change. But as children, all we care about is the now, the present, without any regard for what will happen tomorrow beyond our plans to hang out with our friends or how we will persuade our parents to let us out of the house for our favorite past time.

We don't care about the blurs of the past or the future. We don't think about what we should have done differently or about how much we have achieved or not achieved. We don't think about what we need to complete in the coming few years or what our goals should be, and all of that. All of those concerns are simply irrelevant to us as children. Our only concern is the present. When we ask, "What's for dinner?" we don't have to worry about whether there are enough groceries for it or if our parents can afford to make expensive, delicious meals every day.

This makes the present moment very important for any teenager. Your present would define you when you're living in the moment. You want to ensure that you can live every moment to the fullest and are not pulled into the stream of life. You want to try something unique or different, or fulfilling. You don't care about the costs and go do the things that you want to anyway. Have to take a small loan to go watch the baseball tournament? Go ahead, and we'll figure out how to pay it later! There is a reason teenagers are often described as rebellious. We want to disrupt the status quo, not because we can, but because we think so. It is a time of arrogance and thinking that we know too much. That is part of the reason why taking a risk today is seemingly so inconsequential to us. That spending more today won't be that big of a deal since we are wholly unfamiliar with the challenges of adulthood and having to pay your own bills.

Of course, not everyone lives in the moment like that. Some people do not give in to these societal pressures and are simply themselves. They don't care much about "living" and are happy on their own. Even teenagers, at times, are drawn into change and risky behavior by others but tend to rebel in their own way by simply being content where they are, being the good kids they want to be. It is a strange time for anyone, and opportunity is endless. It is the decade we have to enjoy because after that is college and jobs and retirement, and before you know it, your bones give out, and you are getting a free bus pass. We all have a desire to live in the moment because to us, that old age is our inevitable destination, and living life before that happens is what we all strive to do at some point. But see, society catches up to all of us. The blur becomes more real, and the present moment seems to be the best chance of being what you want to be. Why wait for tomorrow when you could do it today?

The people that don't live in the moment have to live with the blur of memories. They have to see their day continue in the same patterns. They don't get to experience the bliss that other people do, and they simply can't help but feel like they're missing out on something. And the truth be told, they are. It is how someone comes out of their shell, do they truly experience life as it should be. Constantly being in your comfort zone is the exact opposite of living life at the moment. Putting yourself out there, doing something different, finding the courage to ask someone out, all these little things matter in the grand scheme of things. When you are at the end of your days, old and brittle, you won't remember that time you sat at home while the others partied, at least not fondly. At that age, our fondest memories are our favorite. After all, what else do we have when we get old? We cannot exactly take a hike or go out camping. At that age, we have to live with the memories we have and the memories we made.

I mean, think about it. How would you like it if you had to live through the same day every day? And no, I'm not talking about some sci-fi film like 'Edge of Tomorrow' or 'Groundhog Day,' where they might be some real stakes at play. I mean living the same boring, monotonous, and unfulfilling day over and over again. You come home from school, or high school, or college, or work, and it is the same routine every time. You relax and wind down, have dinner, maybe talk with a friend or two, watch some TV, and then tuck in for the night before starting it over again. I'm talking about letting the blur be all that there is in your life and not having any sort of relief from the monotony. It simply seems unbearable, doesn't it? When all that is left in your life is living for tomorrow, that tomorrow never comes, ever. It is the cruel irony of life. Our decisions as teenagers are often reckless, regarded as irresponsible, yet they are the decisions that we will remember most fondly, and in the end, living recklessly is exactly what living in the moment truly is about. When you make that plunge, you know what the consequences are going to be, and even if you don't, all that is in your mind is, "Damn the consequences, I am going to do this." This is not some corny motivational speech that I am making here, believe me. This long and drawn out one-sided philosophical discussion has its purpose. We will get to it.

Of course, as adults, this becomes a part of our life. We do our job to pay the bills, and we know that it's a responsibility that we have to hold, the burden on our shoulders that we have to bear. We know that we have to come to terms with the monotony and have to live with it if we want to earn a basic living and live a life of means. We know that we're stuck doing these repetitive tasks because without them, we can't earn, and without earning, we cannot live. Of course, all the money in the world won't matter if you don't spend it on living. There is a difference between life and living, between being in the moment and being part of a repeating cycle, like a conveyor belt, making the goods but never getting to use them. I believe using inanimate objects in my analogies is not the best way to get my point across, but it helps. After all, are we so different from them? We spend our lives earning, and we spend our lives to earn for tomorrow, our children, so their life is better.

But when we are young, we do not have these concerns. We don't need to worry about how life would treat us or about the future impacts and consequences of what we do. We do not care about how our blur might be better or worse. We just care about something different and unique. Something that isn't just like every other day. Something that becomes a moment that we can hold ourselves in. Something that we can fantasize about later, and something that would become more than just a blur. Something that would become a memory that we can reminisce over and remember it when the days of living like there was no tomorrow are long past us, and our minds and bodies are too fragile to consider a repeat of those events.

See, here's the thing. It's not wrong to want to end the blur. I mean, if you keep trying to live your life the same day every day, you will have nothing different in your life. You will not be creating any new memories. You will be stuck on the same day every day. It can lead to horrible, even frightening outcomes. Depression, anxiety, and other conditions can both be caused by, and are symptoms of, this repeating cycle.

Memories are one of the most important parts of your life. You need to go and ensure that you do something in your life that is memorable to you. Memories are what make your day special, and memories are what you can hold onto when you have nothing else. Memories are what carry you through the worst of your times. They help you remember who you are and what you live for. Memories have always been something that I have cherished and are a part of the reason why I'm writing this book. It is full of my memories, good and bad, and I wish to share them with you. The bad ones help us grow, help us become better persons as we experience the world around us. The good ones can be a reassurance that if life was this good once, it can be that, or even better, once again. Some memories, well, they are just that, memories. No lessons, no great big moral decision to make, just a series of bad ones that be a hoot to think about years later, no matter the situation. Even these confused memories in the middle of the good and bad spectrum have their value. I want to show you how much more there is to life than living the whole day over and over again. It will acquaint you with my experiences, and trust me when I say I have experienced it all, I mean I have experienced it all.

But see, there are also times when we carry the need to make memories too far. There are times when we don't want to live with the blur and make bad decisions that would come to haunt us later. They're memorable, sure, and you definitely might be laughing at yourself 20 years down the line. But at the moment, they are nothing short of terrifying. And those are some of my less proud memories, but I'll still give you guys a short glimpse into them to help you understand them and my perspective of what happened.

See, the end goal of life would be to experience whatever we can and enjoy ourselves while doing it. What's the point of a life that's restricted to your four walls? What's the point of a life that you will spend doing the same thing day after day? The true meaning in life comes with variety, change, but not without the knowledge that things will go back to normal. It comes with doing what you love and experiencing new and unique things. And most importantly, it comes with doing something that we'll enjoy and going down paths that are all flowers and rainbows to us, knowing that we have to go home soon. This variety brings us to a sort of high, and we feel euphoric. There has to be a voice within us that acts as the straight man, the voice telling us that moderation is just as important. If all you have are memories that give you an adrenaline rush, they become less and less exciting every time.

There's a catch to this, too, though. We can't truly know what we will enjoy until we actually do it. And a lot of the time, the things that you think you'll enjoy are not exactly the things that end up giving you any form of joy. They actually end up haunting you and making life a living hell for you.

These crazy things are exhilarating. They give you all forms of thrill, and you can't help but want more of it. You want the adrenaline rush to flow through you and to experience this thrill. You want to get more of it, and you end up doing crazier things. It is like a never-ending downward spiral. There is no beginning or end, and what was once off limits becomes as easy as breathing for you.

This was what happened to me as well. The lines between the joys of life and the risky thrills got blurred, and I ended up getting caught up in the middle of things that I should never have been caught up in. I got myself into trouble while trying to live in the moment, and boy, I tried to live quite dangerously.

However, it did create memories. It did let me do things that I have never done before, and it allowed me to experience life. It was obviously no fun when I was going through it, but it allowed me to accumulate new experiences and gain new perspectives in life, as often is the case for the moments that smack you on the head, some of which you'll be reading through.

I truly did feel that way. I felt that I needed to live in the moment, and well, I naturally went to a party. Of course, when it comes to parties, there is booze, and when you come to a party, you surely have to drink that booze. Now, I do not know, remember, or care to remember what I drank. All I knew was that by the time I left, I was hammered. Basically, the partying turned to drink, and the drinking turned into DUI. And before I knew it, I was caught up in the moment and got myself into trouble. Now, you see, a DUI – or driving under the influence — might not seem too bad when you are just a teenage kid. You might think that the police might understand, even if you are caught, that you are just a teenager looking to have fun. No. DUIs are serious and do lead to criminal charges due to the dangerous and lethal consequences of drunk driving.

This was not the last time that I was going to find myself in that kind of trouble, though. Throughout my life, I was caught DUI under a number of incidents, and it was different each time. You see, the first time doing anything is always terrifying, but as you get used to it, you forget to do certain things. I remember that when I learned to drive, I had to keep in mind where the brake was when I had to put my foot on the clutch and how I had to lightly let go as I went up in speed. Soon it became second nature. At times, if I try to remember how to turn the stick to switch gears, I forget. But, when I'm driving, it comes naturally. I don't ever think that I have to change gears; I just do. You see, the line between normal and anything but gets blurred, and that is exactly what happened here. My first time getting caught with a DUI was terrifying, but now I knew what would happen, and my mind got desensitized to the ordeal. That's what this chapter will explore. A few of the times that I was DUI, and how the circumstances were different each time.

As it might have been obvious by now, I definitely did enjoy the life of partying. I made plenty of friends in the process and obviously got drunk a lot of the time. A few of those times, I also drove. I didn't always get caught, but I did have some DUI tickets, which added fascinating diversity to my career of shenanigans.

The first time that I ever got caught DUI? April 27, 1996. I was in my junior year of high school and thought it would be fun to go party at my classmate's place. He was a jock named Matt, and we weren't particularly close.

That didn't stop me from partying the way I wanted to, though, and we had soon shared several beers. It was then that someone suggested that we should go up to the tanning salon on Mack Avenue.

The influence of the beers was obviously still heavy. I readily agreed to go through with the plan, even though I had nothing to gain from it. I was going to be the one to drive. The drive went without an incident. I had a senior, Joe , and Matt with me. We went to and used the tanning beds. So far, so good. It was time to drop Matt off and call it a night.

Matt lives in the neighborhood of Grosse Pointe Woods. Now, that neighborhood is known for pulling people over, and while we should have, we never really gave it a second thought. How could we? We were drunk and tired, ready to go home to our beds. The reputation was evidently well deserved, though. As you might have guessed: we were pulled over.

I was definitely DUI. I had a hand over my eye to help me with the double vision, and I was practically weaving through the neighborhood. There was no denying it, and I knew that we were in trouble the moment that we pulled over. Nothing could save us now.

Sure as hell, I got arrested. I was charged with driving under the influence in Grosse Pointe Woods. Matt and Joe were charged for Minor in possession, and their parents were called. They were then sent home. My father was called in as well, and he had to come to pick me up in the middle of the night. The eerie silence that shadowed the trip back home still remains clear in memory. He was obviously displeased. The best scolding your parents can give you is silence and disappointment. The guilt along the ride home was enough for me to want to get in my room, lock it, and never come out again. It was not like those times that my parents would guilt trip me into doing things for them. This was serious. I should have learned my lesson then, but as you know, the story — unfortunately — goes on.

If anything, though, it definitely taught me a different kind of lesson. Now I knew what to do, and I knew what to avoid, when to drive while drunk, and when not to. My little foray into a DUI stop made me quite adept at hiding my alleged drunkenness. I was not caught driving under the influence for a long time after. Well, eight years, to be specific. March 18, 2004. That's when I was charged with my second DUI.

Back in March 2004, I was dating a girl named Teresa. I worked at a restaurant called Fishbone's in downtown Detroit, and the shift was, well... not exactly fun. I needed to add more spice to my life. What better way to do so than celebrating St. Patrick's Day?

I made my way to the Irish Pub, the *"Old Shillelagh,"* which was across the street. They were hosting a huge event there, and I was all pumped about it. They had enclosed their parking lot with tents, and there were live bands, food, and keg beer. It was essentially an all-you-could-ask-for buffet, and I was not going to miss out on it! Plus, it was an Irish Pub. What can you expect there but free-flowing booze and some more free-flowing booze for the occasion?

At that time, I used to stay over at Teresa's most nights. She was living at 8 Mile and Mound. She worked at the restaurant Union Street about a mile away from Fishbone's and had a late shift. She would be working till 2 am. The plan involved her staying sober given her late shift, and I would have my fun. Then, she could drive us home and call it a day. I was essentially careful, having learned from my mistake back in 1996.

I did, however, have to drive a mile to pick her up. Now that wasn't exactly risky given how well I knew the route, and I didn't expect to get caught. And thankfully, I did not. However, she didn't exactly stick to her end of the deal. It didn't take me long to figure out that I hadn't been the only one drinking. She had clearly had a few too and hadn't let me have my drinking night by remaining sober. Or well, she had, but it would end up being bad for us.

She later told me that I was simply pissed that she hadn't picked up any weed for me. But that wasn't the case. She was obviously drunk and had not stuck to her end of the deal. It was her drive day, not mine!

But anyway, I was really mad at her and drove off, leaving her outside of the restaurant. I had initially planned on circling around a few times to teach her lesson and then go pick her up again, but I got carried away. I suppose that's what being drunk does to you. I circled around, well, more than a few blocks. Not only that, but I ran a few red lights too. I knew I was in deep trouble by this point, and there was no use running away from it. I was pulled over by the Detroit police, right across the street from the police station. It was a pretty convenient spot. They simply had to walk me across the street and book me for DUI. Pretty straightforward, right?

If only that was that, I would have walked right out. However, I knew that it could mean my car would be impounded. I really did not want that to happen. I knew that if it was impounded, I would have to spend a couple of hundred bucks, and I didn't have that kind of money to spare.

My drunken self thought that the logical move would be to have Teresa come take my car so that I wouldn't get it impounded. Of course, I totally didn't account for the fact that she was drunk too. And now we had two drunk people that couldn't pick the car up, and so the car remained in the legal parking spot across the police station where I had been pulled over.

I was put in the "drunk tank" with the other drunks that had been pulled over on St. Patrick's Day (which there were obviously a lot of). We had to lay on the heated floor and try to sleep the drunkenness off, which, to some extent, did work. However, the news that I heard in the morning made me wish that it hadn't.

One of the arresting officers basically came in to have a chat with me. He suggested that I should break up with Teresa. Now, normally, I would say that that was none of his concern, but he had some more troubling details to share. Apparently, she was saying all sorts of horrible untruths about me while she was at the station. I had mostly forgotten about being pissed at her, but this reminded me of that too. I knew I had to do something about it. I should have ended our relationship right there and then, but I wasn't ready to throw away our relationship just yet. We had been through so much together, it'll make a great read for my next book.

I waited till the morning and knew exactly what I had to do. I had a lot of cash on hand at that time, and while I might have needed it later, I figured that I couldn't exactly do anything with it if I wasn't going to escape this jail anyway. So at 8 am, I paid the bond and bailed myself out of jail. I was now free to go get my car, which at by this point, had been impounded.

I found out that they were keeping my car a few miles down Woodward Street, on which the police station was located. It was a long walk, but I knew I had to make it. I made my way through the cold and arduous journey, only to reach the closed impoundment lot. I stretched my legs and got some rest, waiting for it to open up.

As soon as it did, I presented a few hundred dollars and drove my car off to the only place I could go to: My parent's house. I was not going back to Teresa's place after this. This DUI wasn't all about just the jail, though. I also got a probation period of a year, which I suppose would look great on my growing list of infringements.

I did, however, take breaks between my DUIs. The next time that I was charged with the offense? 2008! It was February of 2008. I was driving through Royal Oak, when I was pulled over and charged for operating a vehicle while intoxicated.

A lot had changed since the last time that I had found myself getting pulled over. I was now 28 and had started a new job. It was at a mortgage company, and I made enough money to consider moving out. In November 2007, I got myself a nice 500 square feet place in Royal Oak, MI. The rent was set at $500, and I was soon moving out.

If there's one thing that comes from moving out, it's loneliness. No one was coming to visit me at this new place, and I didn't know who to meet or talk to. I was basically looking for an escape. So when an opportunity presented itself in the form of a friend's sister's birthday in the city of Mount Clemens, I was overjoyed.

The party also presented an opportunity for me to catch up with some old friends. We went to a bar in Mount Clemens and had fun talking and drinking. At one point, I went outside to smoke weed with my friend Alyssa. She had a bowl on her, and we used it and chatted away. As fun as that was, it turned out to be one huge mistake. Alyssa forgot her bowl in my car, and it ended up getting me in trouble.

I drank the beer and a couple of shots and then went and made my way home. It was late, and I had to drive a good 30 minutes. I almost made it too. I was only two blocks away from my place when a police car started to tail me.

I pulled into the gas station, taking a left, and saw the sirens come on. There was no escape at that point. I knew that I was going to be in trouble. I simply didn't know how much. Now the reason that the cops pulled me over was quite surprising. Apparently, one of my tail lights had gone out, and it was now a crime to drive around town after 2 am with a burnt-out tail light. They assumed it meant I was drunk. I did not humor the connection.

They searched my car and found the conveniently forgotten marijuana bowl. I had to do the roadside test, which I obviously didn't fare too well on. I practically begged them to let me walk away. I lived only two blocks away and had driven a whole 30 minutes! In the end, it came down to the breathalyzer, which I refused. But they had the leverage of the marijuana bowl on me, and I saw no clear way out. They told me they were going to get me one way or another anyway, so I complied.

The jail was not how I had planned to spend my weekend, but I really had no choice in the matter. I was put in on Friday and wasn't able to get out until Monday. Even then, I had to call my boss, Calvin, to bail me out. He was nice enough to do so. I did not want to get my family involved on this one, and they had heard enough about me driving under the influence as it was!

The terms of my release were not exactly lenient. I got my license taken away for five years. I was also put on probation for two years and had to spend a month in jail. The jail was lenient with the prison terms, though, and I had a work release. I could go to work except on Sundays, which were spent brooding in jail.

It wasn't as easy as it sounded, though. See, by this point, I had already quit working at the mortgage place and was considered self-employed. Unfortunately, the work release from jail did not apply to the self-employed, and I was practically stuck in a jail cell for the time being.

In the end, I managed to get some help from a family friend. He added me to his company books, which meant that I now had work release periods as per the company books. I could get out in the morning, but I had to get back to jail in the evenings. At that time, I was dating another girl named Laura.

Laura would pick me up in the morning, and we'd go to my place where I'd sit around or we'd fool around. That was practically all there was to my "work release" time. In the evenings, she would drop me off back at the jail. Those were a difficult few weeks, and I was glad when they ended. This bad experience did end up keeping me away from DUI for quite some time. Almost ten years!

The last time that I was pulled over was in 2017. This happened in July while I was in Austin, Texas, and is perhaps the most interesting of all the times that I have been pulled over for DUI. Just this once, I actually wanted to be pulled over!

Now before you start asking questions about why I would ever want to do that, let me remind you that I'm bipolar. This happened under a manic episode, and I wasn't fully consciously dictating my actions. At that moment, I felt like the star of the show and wanted to be the center of attention. Grandiose behavior comes as a part of bipolar disorder. Well, I suppose I got that wish fulfilled at least!

I had basically smoked some marijuana earlier in the night and had one and a half beers at a bar. I say half, because when I went outside for a smoke, the bartender took my beer and tossed it. I wasn't high on marijuana or alcohol at the time, but I was extremely manic. I left the bar and got into my car. As I pulled out of my parking spot on South Congress I noticed a police car a few yards behind me. Being the happy-go-lucky self that I felt like I was, I pumped at my break twice, practically asking to be pulled over. I was sure to put my license and documents on the roof so that they could know who they pulled over. I did, however, refuse to roll down my window, and danced and showed my middle finger to the cop, which was not helping my case.

Things took a turn for the worse when I finally got out of my car. I knew that I had to do something big to make it memorable, and well, I did. I started walking to the police car parked behind me and threw my hand in the air as if to say, 'what's taking you so long?'

The officer approached me and asked me what was wrong with me. All of a sudden I started shuffling with the cop that had come to arrest me. I really don't know what happened clearly because it happened so quickly. It turns out he was going to pat me down without saying anything to me and I reacted. This was promptly followed by a Taser to my side, which though painful, only elated me more. In a normal situation, I would have gone down like any other person, but given my euphoric mental state and being the ever so temporary king of the world, that was not going to happen just yet. I was tased another time while on the ground.

I tried to wiggle more and was essentially beaten up by seven cops because I refused to comply. They were telling me to put my hands behind my back, but I had them covering my head from their blows. I suggested that I would report them for brutality, and an ambulance was called for me. The drama had unfolded pretty well. The audience must have been very pleased with my performance. I would ask them for a verdict later. Right now, I had an audience that wanted some more hands-on participation.

The cops, however, were not exactly happy with the show that I had put on. They had to put in a lot of effort to get me into the cuffs and had to accompany me for MRI scans as well. Of course, now that I was in the hospital, they were going to test my blood for any substance abuse as well. They hadn't found anything in my car.

A lot followed after, but I'll spare you those details and bring them up again in another chapter. I was put into jail for two months and had five years on probation for having Marijuana in my bloodstream. I think I can be used as an example of why you should not get pulled over on purpose when you have smoked pot earlier in the day.

These are just four of my many run-ins with the law. When you suffer from bipolar disorder and have manic episodes, things are bound to happen. I wasn't always very careful with it anyway, and I have found myself wound up with the system plenty of times because I didn't want to become a part of the blur and wanted to do whatever gave me pleasure. Unfortunately, the pleasures of drinking often come with consequences when you have no one to drive you home.

In the end, I am not proud of myself for getting caught driving under the influence. It's not something that I ever inspired to be booked for (except during the manic episodes), and it was not how I had intended to create my memories. But when you try to create memories, you do have to act a little crazy because it's fun. And when you do the crazy, you do have to get into some crazy run ins with the law.

But I have definitely experienced a lot in the time that I have spent trying to live my life to the fullest. I've partied and gotten pulled over all the way through my adulthood, and from Austin to Detroit to Royal Oak to Florida, Georgia, and Northern Michigan. I've partied plenty and gotten the most out of my life. And I do not regret it one bit.

I have lived life in the moment and in the moments that I wanted to. I have lived with what I loved and have made many wonderful and some not so wonderful memories that I can recount and think of when I'm older. And they have all shaped me into the person that I am today and allow me to stand my manic episodes, and I wouldn't ever want to change that.

With that being said, DUI is definitely not the only rollercoaster that I faced in my life. There are more things that need to be talked about, and that's what the next chapter will focus on: a whole different kind of roller coaster that haunted me throughout my life. So buckle up!

Chapter 6 – Drugs, Eminem, and Dealing with Death

Both of my brothers went to De La Salle High School, but I chose to go to Notre Dame. That's where almost everybody else from my grade school was going, so I figured I'd go where my friends are going too. It's where the guys were going, at least. It was an all-boys school. Notre Dame was right next door to an all-girls school called Regina, and that's where most of us guys found women to date and socialize with. De La Salle didn't have a girl's school next door, and I didn't want to follow in the footsteps of my brothers either. I had heard stories of some of my friends constantly being judged based on how their older brothers or sisters were, which was not a good thing regardless of whether they were troublemakers or not. Scott was a great student, and Justin was terrible, so I didn't need the extra heat from teachers because I wasn't a great student either. I would either always walk in Scott's shadow or be compared to Justin on how being a nuisance 'runs in the family' and whatnot.

I had already started smoking weed, and I had never played football before, but I was a little bummed when I learned that I missed the tryouts. They started in August before school started, and I had no idea they were going on, and I was doing something else like hanging out with friends. Once I found a job later in the year, I never did get to try out for a sports team in high school despite the fact that I excelled at them in grade school. At first, it was because I was too busy smoking weed and hanging out with my friends, and then after that, I was looking for a job and working. Things really started piling up after that, so I rarely ever had time to even consider trying out for sports again.

Our parents set up a carpool where each of our parents would pick us all up and drive us to school for a week, and the parents would rotate. It was me, Brian, Bill, Jason, and Stephen. We would catch a city bus home after school and get dropped off on Mack Ave., just a few blocks from home. Hank lived so far away from us that his father just drove him to and from school.

Homecoming at my high school ended up being pretty messed up for me. I was still dating Lisa Voelker throughout the summer, and I thought everything was good between us. She came to the homecoming game with her friends, and I was there with my friends. We were sitting in different sections, and she got upset because I was not spending enough time with her, so she called me before the dance and told me she wasn't coming. I think she was nervous about going to a high school event when she was still in 8th grade. I had called a few girls as backup, and I was able to get Sarah Nemeckay to go with me. She was one of the girls from my grade school. We went to dinner and to the dance as friends. She was an expensive friend, but a life saver for me. While we were at the dance, Brian wanted to call Lisa and dump her for me. I was capable of doing it myself, but I just think he took joy in being the one that did it, so I let him. I never saw her again.

My old coach Pete invited me to go to Boston with him to watch the Detroit Tigers play the Boston Red Sox. My parents weren't exactly sure, but they trusted me with Pete, so they let me go. Pete already had his ticket, and we drove to the airport together. He purchased a ticket for me right at the window right before departure, so the ticket was around two thousand bucks. He just pulled out a credit card. It was really nice to hang out with Pete because he was generous with his parent's money and always picked up the tab. On one of the flights, we had gotten an upgrade to a first-class ticket, but only one of us could sit in it, and the other had to sit in coach. Pete let me sit in first class just because it was one of my first times on a plane, and I had never flown first class, let alone coach.

When we got to Boston, we checked into a hotel and took cabs all around town. We went to the JFK Library, and Pete gave the cab driver extra money to come back and pick us up at a certain time, but he never showed. We took a tour of the Boston Gardens and were able to look at the locker rooms where so many of the greats and legends in hockey had spent time there. When there was a hockey game at Boston Gardens, they would put the ice on top of the basketball court for the games.

The main reason we were there, though, was to see the Detroit Tigers vs. the Boston Red Sox at Fenway Park, home of the Green Monster. That's the nickname given to the left-field wall at Fenway Park. They call it that because it's somewhere around forty feet tall and only about three hundred feet from home plate. The wall was part of the original construction, and its proximity to the home plate necessitated that height. Pete and I took in a 3-game series of baseball and had a great time there.

Dan and I went downtown one weekend early in the school year to see a band at St. Andrew's Hall, and since neither of us could drive yet, his father Dennis drove us and dropped us off. After the show, we were to call him, and he was going to pick us up. We ended up leaving the concert early and went to a nearby Greek restaurant called Nikki's and grabbed ourselves a booth. We ordered a beer, and the waiter didn't card us. Dan had heard they were lax on asking for an ID, and that's the whole reason we were there. The waiter brought us our beers, and then a little later, he brought us some mixed drinks too. By the end of the night, we were doing shots of Ouzo with the waiter! Dan called Dennis to pick us up, and he was there 20 minutes later. I sat silently in the back seat of the minivan and began to nod off. Before I knew it, I was in front of my house, and Dan was waking me up to get out of the van.

I went into the house and immediately headed for the Lazy Boy chair, where I sat down and reclined it all the way. I began to doze off but then realized I had to throw up and ran into the kitchen. I was throwing up this dark chocolatey substance, and my mother came from behind out of nowhere and started asking me what was wrong. The Ouzo made my puke dark, so she was worried. She said she had thought I had fallen asleep with chocolate in my mouth, however ridiculous that sounds. Suffice it to say; I was caught and punished for getting drunk.

The first time I took LSD is a little blurry to me, but I do remember this one time when Chris and I went out after school with a senior named Mike. Mike dealt in weed and LSD, and I just felt cool hanging out with him. I was a freshman and Chris was a sophomore, and Mike was a senior. The three of us went to Mike's house, and we watched him cut a sheet of acid. He had cut me a strip from the side of the sheet and handed it to me.

The three of us tripped our asses off together, and time went by so quickly. All of a sudden, I had to go home around 9:30 pm. This was the first time I was around my parents while tripping on acid, so I was trying to be on my best behavior. My parents were in the living room watching TV, and I came and laid down on the floor to watch too. I was doing well for a little while, and then something funny came up on TV, and I just lost it. I was laughing for such a long time, and I couldn't stop. When I finally did stop, I noticed both of my parents staring at me like I was crazy, and my mom said, "Looks like somebody's been blowing some dope." When I finally stopped, I was so high, and I didn't know how long I'd been laughing for. It could have been a really long time. I excused myself shortly after and sat in my bedroom, looking at my hand. My parents just thought I was high on weed. At the very least, I could deny being just high on weed, so that was a plus.

Later in the year, Dan and his parents were going to bring a camper down to Myrtle Beach, South Carolina, for spring break, and Dan had invited me to come along. We prepared for the trip by each securing a quarter ounce of weed and some hits of LSD. As soon as we were at the campground, we went around to some nearby stands that were selling weed pipes, and we picked ourselves out new gear. Dan bought a dugout, which is a small wooden box that holds weed and a one-hitter. It's a good choice because it's very convenient. I opted for a wooden box type of pipe that had a chamber in the middle that you could store your weed in to collect resin. Mine wasn't bad but nowhere as good as Dan's.

The campground was a little bit away from the main strip in Myrtle Beach, so we had to get dropped off by Dennis. As soon as we got out of the van, we took our hits of acid. We wandered around trying to collect ourselves before we finally decided to go through Ripley's Believe It or Not Museum. It was a pretty crazy experience tripping through that museum. We did some bungee jumps after that. I don't know many people would agree to take LSD before they bungee jumped, but Dan and I were two of them, always pushing the envelope. The jump was amazing!

One of my classmates, Roderick, worked at a pizza place I had never heard of called Jets Pizza. I asked him if he could get me a position there, and he told me he'd put in a good word for me. I was 15 years old, and other than delivering newspapers and bussing tables at Captain's II, I didn't have much experience. I started at the bottom, and I learned all the ropes with the cutting and rolling dough and making pizzas. I learned the recipes for the sauce and dough, and I knew all the prices for everything, including the tax. My weekends were pretty much shot because those are the busiest nights for the pizzeria, so they needed all hands on deck.

Another time I was tripping on LSD was when I got arrested for possession of weed. My uncle Tom and I were close when I was younger, and we would hang out when we could. Tom, Hank, and I were going to see a movie, so Hank and I took the tabs before my uncle picked us up from my house on Cadieux, and we decided to go to a theater closer to his house. There's usually less riff-raff at the theater the further you get from the city, so we went to a theater out in the suburbs. I had brought a bag of weed with me and rolled a joint for us to smoke before the movie. When the movie was over, and we were in his car, I asked him to stop at a nearby party store in Clinton Township. I walked into the store with a lit cigarette between my lips, like a knucklehead, and there was a policeman at the counter that took notice of me. I tried to avoid him and leave the store, but he was on my ass. He went to grab into my shirt pocket to pull out the pack of cigarettes, and he pulled out my bag of weed too. He said, "Do you know what I hate most about teenage smokers?". Just as he said that he pulled them both out, the cigarettes and the bag of weed, and he turned me around and cuffed me, and then read me my rights. They never did put me in a cell but rather had me sit in the waiting area until my mother arrived.

Ryan was staying at Thom's house, who was an old boyfriend of his mother. Dan, Ryan and I would hang out there quite often, and while Thom wasn't always around, he was cool with us being there so much. Dan lived right across the street, and I was around five hundred feet from him on Cadieux, so it was ideal for us, not to mention that there was pool, pinball, and other arcade games. We would spend some nights there, passed out and drunk. Thom was great, but he was just as shady. He owned Harvard Auto Finders, a company where he and a partner would find specific cars for people. He also likely sold pills and other drugs on the side.

One day, as Ryan was going through one of Thom's closets, he found a large Kenwood speaker box. Going through Thom's stuff was nothing new for Ryan, so finding a speaker ignited his curiosity. Expecting to find a speaker in the box, Ryan found two large bags instead. They were zip-lock freezer bags, and they were filled with weed. The next few weeks for us were spent high 24/7, and still we could not burn through the stash fast enough. We rolled and smoked one joint after the other, and we got so lazy that we did not even bother breaking the buds up. Feeling generous, Ryan even gave a bit away, but that just took a small chunk of his stash.

An acquaintance of ours, Wilbur, or Wimpy as his sisters called him, lived around the block from my old house on Kensington. I saw a record of Michael Jackson's Thriller in his bedroom back in '84, but we had not spoken since then. Ryan, however, did, and he knew that Wilbur had a scale with him that he could use to weigh the weed he had. So, Ryan went to his house, got his weed weighed at 7 ounces out of 2 pounds, which had 32 ounces before Ryan burned through most of it. Tom might have noticed the weed, or might not have, we never got to know that, because the next day it was Wilbur who paid Ryan a visit. He and a few of his buddies pistol-whipped Ryan and threatened him until he gave up both his own stash and that of Thom in the Kenwood box. They had put a bag over his head, Wilbur's friends shouting that they should shoot Ryan, and kept taking the bag off. When he finally gave up the location of the stash, they rushed upstairs and left as abruptly as they came in. Ryan prayed to God that day.

Ryan told Thom about the robbery, but said nothing about him smoking any of it. In fact, Ryan said nothing about weed, just that some guys broke in their home and stole the Kenwood speaker box. After a brief conversation with Thom and a visit to the emergency room, Ryan found out that Thom's stash was not some run-of-the-mill street peddling weed, but was some high-end stuff, top-of-the-line. Those 2 pounds would have been worth around $6,000-$8,000, and Thom owed it to some guy named Romeo. Now, Romeo was huge, like a football player, so Thom did pay him the amount. Romeo paid a visit to Wilbur too, and while his friends got away, Romeo was able to extort his family for a while. It was quite an ordeal. Ryan came out unscathed from it as well.

Cedar Point Amusement Park was open for the summer, so Dan and I had planned to make the three-hour drive down to Sandusky, Ohio, but we first needed to procure some beer and acid to bring with us. We filled up a cooler with ice and went off to the Liquor store to find somebody to buy us some beer. We learned that this was the best way to get a beer if we couldn't find anybody to do it for us. We got somebody to get the beer for us and gave him a tip, and then hit the road. When we arrived at our hotel, Dan had to use a fake ID that said he was 18 to rent the room because he was 16 and I was 15. We checked into our hotel room and carried our cooler filled with beer up the stairs.

We took the acid that we brought and made our way to the amusement park. The beer we brought would be for after the amusement park when we get back to our room. We went on all the rides they had to offer and tripped balls. I don't know why I do these things to myself. Our hotel was about 15 minutes from the park, so when we had had enough of the rides, we found Dan's car in the massive parking lot and made our way back to our room. After being around all those people at the park while tripping, it was nice just to get away from them, so I could let loose.

Those beers were ice cold after sitting in the cooler for so long, and it sure made them go down easily. We smoked some weed on the stairwell outside of our room and tried to figure out what to get into next. There was a go-cart place across the street from the motel, and we decided we were going to ride them. Maybe six beers deep, LSD, and some weed, and we were going to drive go-carts. We got across the street and made our way to the desk area to talk to the clerk. Surprisingly, the guy didn't ask for any ID to drive the carts, so we both paid and got in our go-carts. It was exhilarating, and neither of us died, so I call that a good trip.

My family had planned a reunion in Colorado that summer, and Justin wasn't able to come with us because he was on-call to take an exam to become a fireman. We went down to Steamboat Springs, Colorado, and had our family reunion. It was nice to have almost all of us together. My grandfather Edmund had just died the previous year, so my grandmother Rita decided not to come for some reason. His brothers Chester and Leo and his sister Charlotte and their families were all there, though. My second cousin Dan was there too, but since he's a few years younger than me, we were worlds apart. I was drinking and smoking weed, and he was still into dinosaurs.

My father's cousin Matt, which is my first cousin once removed, took Scott and me to a Stone Temple Pilots concert at the Red Rocks Amphitheater. That was the highlight of the trip for me. Matt said we would be able to get tickets outside of the venue, and he was right. We bought some scalped tickets for the three of us and went in. Matt had made jungle juice and put it in a big thermos-type container. Jungle juice is a variety of liquor and a variety of juices all mixed together. Sometimes people put fruit in it. The batch he made was good and strong, and once we found some seats, we passed the thermos around.

I had brought a bag of weed with me and was down to my last joint. Up until then, I would just sneak away by myself and smoke a joint. I brought my last joint to the concert and pulled it out. Matt was happy as hell. Scott's not a smoker, so after he hit it a few times, he fell asleep during the concert. It was an awesome show for us, though. I kept slamming that jungle juice, and before I knew it, I had drunk too much, and I was toast. I fell asleep quickly on the drive home and slept the whole drive. That was the highlight of my reunion.

Scott, Matt, and I went hiking at a local mountain. Matt had hiked it a few times before. We packed the cooler with some ice and beer but not much water and made our way there. About two miles in, we're walking and walking, and the water bottles go dry. Scott and Matt are both super competitive, so they want to keep going until we reach this lake that Matt has been at before. I'm dying and ready to quit, but I keep going, and we finally reach the lake. There were two nude women swimming in the lake by themselves, so we decided to grab a seat and take in the scenery. The way back to the car was just as bad on me. I was hot, sweaty, tired, and as thirsty as I've ever been in my life. Once we got back to the car, Scott and Matt cracked some beers, and I ended up drinking the ice that had turned to water in the cooler. I was 15 and didn't like the taste of beer yet, but dirty cooler water was just fine.

Matt brought us to a natural hot spring on one of the days out in the middle of nowhere. The drive got scary down those dark winding roads. A few times, Matt turned off the headlights and scared the shit out of us. Pitch darkness all around, and the only light visible was coming from the stars and moon, which were so bright and illuminating away from the city lights. When we arrived at the hot springs, there was a whole team of women volleyball players already in the hot spring. They were about 20 years old, so a little too old for me. Scott took some initiative and chatted up the girls in the hot spring but ended up empty-handed.

On Cadieux Road, we became the "cool-aid" house where most all our friends would hang out. My dad had setup a basketball hoop in the backyard with an adjustable rim, which were new at the time. It allowed you to raise and lower your basketball rim. We would lower the rim until we could dunk and we normally played that way. I had been working on a trick shot for a long time before I pulled it out on the court. It was a layup, but my shot was a layup from behind the backboard and I got good at it.

The Jets Pizza was located on 8 Mile and Mack and that was kind of far from my house to be getting picked up all the time, so when I heard another location was going to open near my house, I asked about getting transferred. They didn't want to see me go, but my manager understood it made more sense for me to work at the closer location, so after a year of employment, I was transferred to Mack and University location in Grosse Pointe.

I have the memory of meeting someone that most of us would be familiar with by now; Eminem, Slim Shady, Marshall Mathers, whatever name you would like to give him. There was a house that I would go to with the other guys, Dan, Hank, Ryan, David, and all, on Wayburn Street at Grosse Pointe Park. A few guys lived at that house. There was Mike (Manix) and Matt (D.J. Butterfingers) Ruby, James Deel (Chaos Kid), and Marshall Mathers. Mike Ruby was friends with Marsh in high school and the pair formed Manix & 'M&M' that would later turn into Eminem.

I would go over there often, mostly to smoke weed. In fact, part of the reason they even let us hang out with them at first, was that they needed company to roll and smoke a few joints. They would smoke and rap, listen to music, and smoke some more weed and rap some more too. It was how it all went, day by day, getting high and rapping. That is where I met with Marsh for the first time, too. He was with the rest, Manix and the group, rapping to some beats in the upstairs bedroom. I really like Manix and Chaos Kid the most out of all the guys. They didn't look down at as for being younger than them and they taught us a lot about style.

Among all of them, however, meeting Eminem was the most memorable, partly because I loved his freestyle raps, and partly because of getting to listen to them before he was famous and all that. When we first met, and by that I mean when I first saw him, he was rapping at the house, in the upstairs bedroom. We could hear them rap when we came in downstairs. When we came upstairs, greetings were exchanged, and Manix, Butterfingers, and the group handed us a joint, and told us to pass it around. We did bring our own, that was the whole point of us being there, but they were generous enough too. Dan thought he could sing along with them, but if you know how fast Eminem raps, you can imagine that he could not keep up with them. It was a little embarrassing for us all, at first, but it was quickly forgotten. After some time, when we all mellowed out a bit, we were just vibing to the music.

Now, anything from Bassmint Productions and their original EPs are some of the most sought out collections from Eminem's fans. There was also the fact I got to see what came to be Bassmint Productions and the origins of Soul Intent, some of heralds of Detroit's Golden Age of hip hop and rap music. I remember when Marshall Mathers and I first spoke. It was a quiet night. We had all decided to hang out at the house in Grosse Pointe Park. I had been there a few times before, with Marshall present, but we never really spoke one on one, even in passing. This one time, however, the group was rapping as normal, trying out their freestyles, different tunes on the same lyrics, different lyrics on the same tunes and all that. I generally did not listen much, but this time, I think, things were a bit different.

Usually when I got to the house, the party was already blowing in full, and there was a lot of passing around. We were not early today, they just started late. The singing and the music had not started yet, so we had a bit of time to talk to everyone. So we all started talking to each other, and while Ryan and Hank talked to Manix, Dan and I talked to Marshall Mathers. It started with Marshall asking the both of us what we did. You know, small talk. We would usually hang out and smoke weed, so there was not much in terms of getting to know each other. Right now, the pair of us and Marshall were talking about what we all did, what we liked to do, the goals we were pursuing, and all that. It is not very different to how anyone else would act like when being introducing oneself to someone else. In fact, it was quite mundane. You would expect that meeting what was to be a future superstar would be something grand, but it was not to be so. At the time, he had a shaved head and everybody called him Marsh. He seemed a little timid to me and didn't quite feel comfortable in his own skin yet.

Well, not long after, we were smoking and rapping again. This time, I paid more attention to the words, the lyrics, and boy they were vulgar. I realized that I got so high in between coming to the house and leaving, that the beats that everyone rapped to were the ones I remembered more than the words spoken. I guess that is why these tracks were unreleased, decades in the future. It would be quite controversial to get them out there now.

I had been working throughout the summer as the night shift manager and by the time my sophomore year started, I had become store manager at the age of 16. They never asked for my age and I never gave them one. I had done what most 16 year olds in my shoes what have done; I hired my friends to come work with me. Hank was working at Kroger's grocery store and he wanted to earn some extra money as a delivery driver, so I hired him and his brother Reggie needed a job, so I hired him and his friend Felix too. Ryan had been working at a Jet's pizza near his house at 10 Mile and I-94 freeway, but needed a job after he and his boss had gotten into a big argument. It became like a hangout that we did work at some time. There was also a ton of weed being smoked outside of the building. For weed, we would drive to a street called French Road and there would be a few guys standing around. One would run up to your car and ask you how many dime bags you wanted. You'd give him an answer and hand him your money. He'd run off to where he has his stash hidden and come back to the car with it. I'd say it's about 97% safe.

When the school year began, I had to work out an agreement with Derrick, the owner, so that I was only working 40 hours per week. We agreed on a salary of $400 per week take home and he would handle the taxes separately. Not too shabby for a 16 year old! The schedule was made by me, so I took Fridays off so that I could hang out with Missy. I worked every other night of the week and a double either on Saturday or Sunday.

Leaving nobody apparently in charge while I was out on Fridays proved to be a mistake. I later found out that my bozo friends would take the phones off the hook when they started getting overwhelmed. Imagine trying to call a pizza place over and over and you just get the busy signal. I'm sure all kinds of money was lost. We never had to take the phones off the hook when I was there. Lucky for my friends, they didn't tell me this until years later, because I most likely would have had to fire them.

One Friday night, I was hanging out with Missy and I got a call from the pizza joint. It was Rob, a kid I had hired to work at my Jets. He and I were coworkers at the 8 Mile store and he wanted to work closer to his house too, so I hired him. Rob had a smart aleck mouth and it would irritate people, so I wasn't too surprised at the story he relayed to me. Ryan punched him in the mouth during the pizza rush hour with a room full of spectators in the lobby.

Rob was making the pizzas and Ryan was cutting them during the rush. Rob felt so busy that he could not put in the Jet Breads for the orders that called for them and this was pissing Ryan off. The lobby was filled with people waiting on their pizzas when Ryan confronted Rob about not putting the Jet Breads in the oven and that's when Rob said something smart to Ryan to piss him off. Ryan slapped Rob in the face in front of a room full of patrons and Rob ran out the back door.

I wasn't going to fire my lifelong friend, Ryan, even though he was in the wrong. Sure it was stupid for Rob to just put the pizzas in the oven and not the Jet Breads to complete the orders, but Ryan had no right to slap him either. It was difficult to leave those guys unsupervised after that affair

As manager at Jets, I was responsible of the hiring and firing of employees, creating the weekly schedule, ordering products, counting the money at the end of shifts, and delegating the work out to the employees. I had a day shift manager named Don that would handle the food preparation and lunch rush from the Grosse Pointe South high schoolers. Don was a black guy in his 50's or 60's and I oftentimes felt awkward giving him orders to carry out, like mopping the floor.

At Notre Dame High School, we had these raffle tickets we were supposed to sell to our family members and friends of our family's to raise money for the school. As an incentive to sell the tickets, if a student met their quota, they'd get certain Fridays off from school. Hank and I never bothered with selling the tickets, and on those Fridays, it would just be him and me in some of our classes by ourselves. It wasn't worth the pestering of our family and friends to us. It kind of felt like a multi-level scam trying to get people to help our school by selling raffle tickets.

From what I can recall from Brian's story is that he called his grandparents over to his house on April 11, 1997, to buy some of these raffle tickets. When they came to his house in Grosse Pointe, they couldn't find him in the house and ended up in the basement where they had found that he had hung himself. I guess Brian had some demons he was battling and had been molested at the age of 13 or 14 by somebody at the golf course where he worked as a caddy. He and I weren't as close as we once had been, so he never confided any of this information to me, but I believe he did with some of his closest friends.

For the week that I had been out of school on our trip to South America, the whole school had also been out of class. Everybody was dealing with their grief over Brian's death. It was a surreal experience for me because I felt strange that I had missed this event, and everyone else had a week's head start on dealing with their emotions. I had heard that the church was filled to the rafters with people. Hank had told me that he was with Brian the day before he committed suicide, and they had smoked some weed together. I don't recall one time ever smoking weed with Brian, so this seemed out of the ordinary to me.

I had missed no schoolwork while I was gone, so I had no assignments to make up for. I had missed Brian's funeral, and I had missed grieving with the rest of my classmates. It was and is still to this day a crazy feeling. Hank and I still had to come to school on those Fridays, though, for not selling our raffle tickets.

May 17, 1997, I graduated from high school at Notre Dame by the skin of my teeth. I was a consistent 'C' student throughout school. One of my teachers, though, Mr. Vachon, who hated my guts because I fell asleep in his class often, gave me an 'F' my senior year. I never memorized the monologues he wanted us to, and we just clashed. He loved my friend Brad Marx though. I don't think I was technically even supposed to graduate due to some rule they had about failing a course in your last semester, but I made it somehow. For about half of my time at high school, I was working 40 hour weeks at Jets. The other half, I was high on weed.

While working at Jets, I had saved up enough money to get my first car. My parents matched me dollar for dollar, and I bought a used red Volkswagen Fox that my dad had picked out after doing some research. It was a four-door with a stick shift, and it wasn't anything too fancy, but I was happy with it. I had already learned to drive a stick shift with Missy's Ford Escort. She would let me drive her car sometimes and taught me to use the clutch, so I got that out of the way. That car ended up giving me a lot of problems, though.

Two weeks after I graduated, I had parked my Volkswagen Fox across the street from our house on Cadieux, and some lady was driving down the road and crashed into my car, totaling it. She had a child with her in the car and was rushed away in an ambulance before we could get her insurance information. Sure enough, it turned out she didn't have any insurance, and she dodged every court summons to get her to pay something for ruining my car. I was carless for a good year after that.

The summer after I graduated, I threw a party at my house while my parents were out of town. A fight broke out fairly shortly into the party between two people I did not recognize, and the backyard was booming too, so the neighbors called the cops. When they showed up, everyone scattered off and ran to their cars or through Messmer park behind my house. Only a few of us were left behind cleaning up, and my brother Scott's friend Sean Rivers was one of those people that didn't need to run. He was already 23 years old, so he was trying to diffuse the situation with the police, but there weren't having any of it. Being the resident, they wrote me a noise complaint because I was causing a disturbance. They said I would have to appear in court for a hearing. I couldn't believe it.

I went to my court date in Detroit, and the judge sentenced me to 40 hours of community service just for throwing a party! I was told to report to the janitor at the Eastern campus of the Wayne County Community College on Conner Street and pretty much to follow orders. I really didn't want to do gross things like clean toilets just because I had some people over my house, so I was really anxious about showing up that first day.

I showed up and looked for the guy that's going to tell me what to do. I noticed a man off in the distance, a military-style look about him. I approached him and told him my name. He brought me to the janitor's workspace area and sat down. The janitor said to me, "If you go to McDonald's right now and buy me a large Big Breakfast meal, I'll sign your sheet for you, and you can go home, and you won't have to do any work at all. Just come to me when your time is up, and I'll fill out all the paperwork for you".

The 40 hours of free work I was dreading turned out to only cost me $7 worth of a McDonald's breakfast, and I was a free man. I'm glad I brought cash that day. When I went to see him one other time to pick up my completed paperwork, he told me that sometimes people give him a tip for letting them off the hook. I searched my pockets, and I gave him $30 or $40, and he seemed really pleased with that, and I know I was as well.

Chapter 7 - Love is a Smoke Made with the Fumes of Sighs...

Love is perhaps one of the greatest mysteries of life. It takes you by the hand and can take you anywhere, on adventures and the most incredible days of your life. When in love, everything feels right, and the world feels like a great place to live in. When it is taken away, you never really let go. It is snatched from you. Love or loss, it always leaves you a little more sober, regardless of what happens. It is one of those emotions that cannot be analyzed, as it is a bit different for everyone. But, some things love does that everyone gets to know one way or another.

Sooner or later, love leads to loss, and everyone experiences it. Those that don't, well, they are singlehandedly, the luckiest people on this earth. Some say loss and hurt are just part of love and life that we miss out on if we don't experience hurtful breakups, slowly drifting apart from the ones we used to be close with, eventually becoming so distant that the connection we had is lost. It can prepare you for your life ahead, in a way, but that does not make the experience altogether pleasant in the slightest.

Sometimes I wonder how something can be so wonderful and so hurtful that it is not easy for me to understand or even grasp, and I have always struggled with its idea. At times, I feel like I am finally living, achieving stability that I cannot describe, nor could I ever explain. At times, that same feeling leads to bouts of loneliness, and it feels like my body and soul are drifting apart. It is a feeling of nothingness, a sort of numbness, almost like I have insomnia. I feel like I am never really anywhere, floating and running through life at once, staying still but speeding through the days without any rhyme or rhythm, lacking any purpose whatsoever.

Moments seem to burn into moments, then. All I could ever do in these situations would be just to sit down and sigh. It helped calm me down. I have had quite a few run-ins with this enigmatic force over the years. I feel like I have matured, having experienced almost anything and everything, and I think I pretty much have my love life sorted out by this point. And by sorted out, I mean I don't know how to make heads or tails of it.

Honestly, it started pretty simple. It always does, and when it gets serious, it catches you off guard. Now that I think about it, grade school was all innocent and hurt-free crushes that didn't take a toll on me. It was…easier back then. All I remember from my earlier childhood are the great memories, the feelings of crushing on girls without thinking of spending my future with them. All that was on my mind at that time was the now, the present. I think I was dating this girl named Jacklyn that I played house with in kindergarten. It was all innocent. So much so that I have very little to tell you about it. I have some good memories of her, but that is all.

Hillary and I used to fool around at a young age, but I wouldn't quite call her a crush. I don't know how or when we started playing "doctor" in her attic whenever we got the chance, but it still baffles me. You see, playing doctor has all sorts of interesting things happen. If you get sick, the only cure for it was kissing. It involved a lot of kissing and nakedness. Soon though, we got too old to play doctor, and it was time to drift apart there as well.

My second crush after that was back in school was when I was only six years old. I honestly don't remember much about the girl, except her first name, which is also a maybe, although the only reason I remember her name is how she always used to correct me on it. I think she was named Lindsy or Lindsay. It was one of those two, I'm sure of it. There is nothing much to say beyond that. The third crush that I had was much more memorable. I don't remember it like it was yesterday, but I remember a lot more than either Lindsey or Jacklyn. This crush was on a girl named Emily.

I'm pretty sure I wasn't the only one that was crazy after her. She was like that. Emily was one of those people that would just fit in anywhere, and everyone loved her. Emily would make my heart flutter, and I did go out of my way for her. I guess most people did. I mean, I even joined the school choir just because she was in it! Now, I'm very tone-deaf in my singing, and I don't care much about it, but being in the choir allowed me to see more of Emily. I was not exactly a prodigy, but I was not terrible either. I was just good enough to get by, unnoticed by the choir teacher, though I could say the same for Emily as well. I did notice occasional glances towards me, but that was only when the teacher was calling out our names. I suppose that was enough to keep me going. Sadly, that crush never really went anywhere. It was just that. Emily moved away in the third grade, and I understood that I needed to move on as well.

This time around, I started crushing on this girl named Shavon. And by crushing, I mean obsessing. I liked her, but she hated me. At least I think she did. Nope, I'm pretty sure she did hate me. At that time, Shavon did a lot to indicate she wasn't even remotely interested in me. Luckily, now that Emily had left, it meant that I no longer had to be a part of the choir, which was great because I don't think it is in many children's interest to be a choir boy. I decided to join the boy scouts instead. I think this was the start of my journey in sports, though ultimately that too, never went anywhere beyond grade school. It was much better than being stuck in a room shouting. I'd take pinewood derby racing over singing at the top of my lungs any day!

I managed to engage myself in sports quite a bit, which was a great decision for me. I wasn't some childhood prodigy that would get any sort of career out of it, but it was worth it. As a kid, I had a lot of free time, as most of us do, and I tried my hand at almost everything. I got onto the basketball team, our baseball team, and tried my hand at soccer, though that one was far more casual than the other two. I played basketball and baseball to win. Soon after that, I became the captain of all of our basketball, soccer, and baseball teams. I became one of the most popular kids in school. Despite all that, however, Shavon still didn't as much as look at me, which was kind of hurtful. In the 8th grade, I finally got something out of her now, as I remember it, that something was just a game of spin the bottle that got me a kiss from Shavon! It isn't as exciting now and might not seem like it to anyone looking back at it, but the 8th-grade child I was at that time was nothing short of ecstatic.

The chronicles of Shavon came to an end though, and boy, was that a thrill ride. If you have not picked up on it, I am sarcastic right now. She was dating my friend, Brian, and I knew I stood no chance with her. This chronicle was short, barely having anything of note, with the most exciting event being a smooch I got. I learned that spin the bottle only gets you anywhere if the girl likes you too, and knowing Shavon, I was a fly on the wall that was not even worth swatting away. I know I shouldn't compare myself like that, it's not exactly healthy, but I felt this at that time. I tried everything for Shavon, and by not acknowledging my existence, she hurt me in her way.

When I went to California for that year in 4th grade, I soon developed a crush on another girl named Aimee. She was a blonde with blue eyes, which made her one of the prettiest girls in my school. It was "love at first sight," at least for me. As soon as I had seen her in the playground, I knew that I wanted her! Unfortunately, she did not share my sentiment, as she was already dating someone at that time. She was Tyson's girl, and he was the most popular kid in school, more so than me. Tyson was the best baseball player the school had and I stood little chance in trying to get noticed under Tyson's shadow. He was a baseball player in my brother's league. He was older than the rest of us, because he had been held back. He was my friend too, so once again, I stood no chance. My crush on Aimee was something she eventually learned about, though I was somehow snaked into dating Aimee's friend instead.

Aimee's friend, Amanda, was not really what I was aiming for, but I was happy with her. Amanda wasn't Aimee, but I wasn't exactly too picky, and I liked her. She was cool. Of course, I liked Aimee better, but hey, I had to take what I got! But anyway, she dated me for a few weeks before she broke up with me and told me she was simply testing to see if I would be the right pick for Aimee. That was quite a punch to the gut, and I cried about that breakup. I had grown fond of Amanda, and I didn't want to break up with her. But well, things happened, and I couldn't change them. The worst part is, I didn't even get to find out if I'm a fit for Aimee or not. Maybe she still hasn't reached a verdict. I remain hopeful.

When I was twelve, I started dating a neighbor of mine named Andrea. We used to kiss a lot, and I got my practice from her. We didn't get to meet that often, even though I did invite her over to the clubhouse quite a few times.

In between Andrea and Suzy there is a small list of innocent girlfriends that I dated for a few weeks and I would feel bad leaving them out. I dated Ann Marie from my childhood and a girl named Regina. They were more a matter of conveniences and experiments rather than love. There was a whole lot of like though!

The next girl that I dated was Suzy. She came over to the junior high building with a bunch of other seventh graders when I was in eighth grade. My friends and I were very pleased and decided to have our pick of girls. My pick was Suzy, and we had a lot of fun times together. However, she decided to break up with me one day for no reason at all. My friends and I all got dumped at the same time! I must say, getting dumped together did not hurt. My friends and I would just laugh about the ordeal. I never asked Suzy why she broke up with me or why it was synced up with her friends doing the same.

After Suzy, I started dating her friend named Lisa. I liked her a lot, and she was very pretty. I dated her through summer and really liked her, and things were going well. However, they took a downwards turn soon enough during the high school homecoming season. We both came to the homecoming game with our respective friends, and we were sitting in different sections. I thought that was cool since we would be going to the dance together later, but apparently, Lisa wasn't okay with it. She got mad at me for not spending enough time with her and told me that she wouldn't be going to the dance with me. Brian ended up calling her and breaking up with her for me. I would have done it on my own, too, but he thought it'd be more fun for him to do it.

Hank and I went to this Catholic youth program to try and meet girls. We met these two friends, named Missy and Jackie, which we both immediately hit off with. I started dating Jackie while Hank was dating Missy. Dating Jackie was a lot of fun. We used to go down to the basement and make out and have fun. However, we also used to argue almost all the time. We lasted a few months before we broke up. I honestly don't even remember who broke up with who anymore. We still hung out, though, and I started getting attracted to Missy. I found out that the feeling was mutual. She liked me as well. The problem was that she was dating my best friend, Hank.

I don't like what I did, but well, I started to do things with Missy. She was cheating on my best friend with me, and I couldn't resist her. She was very desirable, and we kept doing things under his nose. See, Missy was the most beautiful girl in her high school, and she was also brilliant, had a good sense of humor, and was a talented musician. How could I ever resist her? How could anyone?

In the end, she got distant from Hank for apparent reasons. Hank came to me for advice, which I wasn't very good at, but I did conveniently ask him if he'd be okay with me dating Missy if the two of them ever broke up. He told me that he couldn't think of a better person for her than me. She did end up breaking with him, and he was mad at me about it. He never said anything about me, though. I knew I was a bad friend to Hank, especially since he was so nice and trusted me. At that time, though, most of my mind was on Missy, and as much as I hate to say it, I couldn't care less about Hank. Of course, we were buddies, but I don't think hormones ever allowed us to think clearly, especially at such a young age when we are discovering ourselves.

Soon after, I started working and set up an arrangement that would allow me to take Fridays off. Fridays were then spent with Missy from thereon. She had a nice place, and I used to go with her to her basement, where she had a couch and a TV. We tried it at my place too, but unfortunately, my mom caught us and I was sent to see the priest. That did not do much good. I remember getting quite a few lectures about being chaste. All that flew over my head. I was head over heels for this girl, so I only went to places I knew my parents wouldn't find me. My mother had sent me to the same priest that had baptized me as an infant.

By this point, I was convinced that I had made the right choice. I liked Missy a lot, and she seemed to return every ounce of that affection. I was truly happy with her even though I felt like a jerk for going behind the back of my best friend, Hank. Missy also had some rich friends that threw parties, and it was plenty of fun! I even got to learn to drive using her Ford Escort.

Another fun trip that we had with Missy's friends was to Cancun, Mexico. I obviously couldn't afford it, but

Missy started to save for me using my paychecks. She'd hold on to a certain sum every time I got paid so that I wouldn't spend all of it. I convinced my mom, so I got some financial help from home too. I was the only one who had to work to pay for my trip, though the rest were from rich families. It was still plenty of fun, though! The resort was great, and we had plenty to drink, even though most of us were seventeen at that time. I was still with Missy when we graduated high school and started our journey to college.

Remember how Missy was all talented and brainy? Well, she landed a scholarship to her dream university, the University of Michigan, which is no easy feat. She was going to accept it, and I had to try to get there with her. I knew it was out of my reach, though, so I opted for the Eastern Michigan University that would accept my average C grade. It did mean that my apartment was only 20 minutes from Missy's, though, so I was delighted. Of course, when things seem to be going all so well, and any hurdles are crossed with relative ease, something is waiting to snatch it all away. I am not this cynical usually, but with Missy, it seems like I was dealt a great hand, and someone came up to the table and flipped it over.

Our college life was too different. Missy was in a great university, and mine was mediocre at best. In the end, Missy ended up joining a sorority called Kappa Kappa Gamma, which made things difficult. You can't allow non-fraternity members to come to the parties. I only ever went a few times as a guest. Most of the time, she went without me. She did try her best to get me in where she could, though. She even sneaked me into a University of Michigan football game against Ohio State!

But well, she had a lot on her plate and was usually always busy, and at places that I couldn't go to. We started to drift apart, and there was no use in trying to save that relationship. Missy simply had too much to do that I had no way of being a part of, and rarely ever getting to meet up did not help our relationship. I knew I had to get over

Missy. The realization that there is nothing you can do when something great with someone happens, and you slowly but surely drift apart is what pain feels like. If a girl who I liked didn't like me back as much broke up with me, it was hurtful, sure, but never like this.

During the summer after my freshman year, I started working at a place called Fishbones, and that's where I met Teresa. She used to work as a waitress at Fishbones.

Teresa was 22 years old and wanted to be an actress. She was trying to get out of a seven-year-long relationship as well and liked the attention that she received. She was learning to be an actress, so she definitely knew how to get some attention as well, and she caught mine.

I wanted to get closer to Teresa, but a lot of guys liked her. I wanted to get some time alone with her somehow, and I often passed by her house to see if she was back home from work or not. This would have been a unique experience for me because Teresa was actually older than me. Also, unlike Missy, she did smoke weed, and I could do it with her instead of just having her watch me while I smoke.

I eventually got to make my move on her when we were on a couch together at her place, watching a movie. I started to massage her legs, and it eventually ended up with us having sex. She was actually experienced, and she knew what she needed. Missy was not like that. It wasn't bad with her at all, just a bit different. Teresa was not shy, and she told me what she needed me to do to her and guided me. I was her ninth sexual partner. I do not know how I feel about that. Number nine. Heh.

Teresa used to come to my apartment initially. But things changed, and then I started dating her, and I used to live with her at her apartment in Detroit. Life was crazy with Teresa and I spent some of the best and worst moments of my life with her over a seven year span. I don't get into the relationship much in this book, but I will be sure to divulge in my next book.

The next girl that I met was Laura. We lasted three and a half years and spent our Christmastimes and other Holidays together with our families. She moved in with me in Royal Oak, shortly after meeting on Match.com. We spent a week at a resort in the Dominican Republic. I had shared a room with her, Justin had a room to himself and my parents had their own room. At that time, Justin was not exactly a great influence, quite the opposite, and while I did get into the serious kinds of drugs with him, smoking weed is one thing, but beyond that is only trouble.

Justin and I started doing cocaine. I was able to score some weed and coke from one of the bellhops at the resort. I did not tell Laura this. We just told her we were smoking weed, which she didn't smoke. This made the cocaine very easy to hide. I had a lot of fun gambling with Justin and even made some money. It was the best cocaine I had ever done. The purity of it blew anything I had ever tried out of the water. Laura, Justin, and I The went parasailing. She had a lot of fun, but I personally felt very scared and thought that I would fall. I don't think I was strapped in correctly and I was just waiting to drop down to the water. Laura went for a second round with Justin while I sat on a boat and watched. We had a lot of fun in the Dominican Republic, but it was soon time to get back home.

When we got back home, Laura started going to her 9 to 5 paralegal job again, leaving little time for me to spend with her during the day. I worked on weed crops through the night. Laura would go to work during the day and we would eat dinner together and spend some time together afterwards. When she went to bed, I would use her car to go to the grow house I was renting in Warren. I'd work through the night and return home in the morning in time for Laura to get to work. It was a crazy cycle I was running through.

July was a difficult month. I planned a trip to a music festival with Laura for her birthday called Blissfest in

Northern Michigan. It was also the month my crop got ready to be harvested, and I simply didn't know how to juggle everything at once. I had more weed than I could trim by myself and I finally had more weed than I knew what to do with.

I had to do something risky and put up a Craigslist ad. I was able to sell $1200 worth of weed to a guy that carried a medical license. That was the most money I had had on me in a long time, and I planned on making the most of it.

However, it was not going to play out as I had imagined that it would. The reason was that I got paranoid, and I began to think that I was under surveillance due to what I had done. It made me act very weird, which Laura and Justin easily noticed as soon as we started our music festival journey. As I said before, I was never exactly great at being subtle.

The music festival went quite well at first. There were some rocky aspects to it, like me not having my shoes and the tent missing a few pieces here and there, but we managed to scrape through and salvage the trip. It sadly didn't last for too long, though, and things soon started to go south after that.

I acted very weird at the festival and was being a little above myself. If you are not familiar with what that means, it was the first of many of my bipolar episodes. My paranoia had led me to believe I was the most important drug dealer the world had ever seen and that 'they' were hot on my heels with a price on my head. Laura felt that something was off, and she and Justin consulted each other and decided that it was best if I headed home the next day. Bless them. I don't think anything positive would have come out of my grandiose adventure.

The rest of the days weren't exactly any better. I was trying to catch the attention of satellites and thinking that fellow festival attendees were following me. Laura even recorded some of it, which serves as a nice memory. I even thought I was Jesus Christ at one point! As you can tell, it was pretty bad. Delusions of grandeur are one thing, but delusions of godhood are another. Laura once told me that I put on a towel at one point, proclaiming it as a robe. It might be funny to some, but being on the wrong end of this makes everything a tad bit serious. I don't mean to bring anyone down, but this can be scary. If you cannot control yourself or your actions, what's next?

My parents didn't know what to do with me since Xanax didn't exactly work. They wanted to help me, but they didn't know-how. So they did what they thought was the best for me and tricked me into going to the hospital. It was Laura's birthday, but she had decided to go back to her parents and not stay with us. That is quite understandable.

I ended up landing in a psychiatric ward where they were going to help me. They had a steady routine that I got accustomed to. Laura and Justin came to visit me on some days and my parents were there every day. On the tenth day, I was authorized for release and made my way back home.

I wasn't exactly completely okay, though. I was still a little over the top, feeling like a little more than I should have been. Laura and my mom tried to help me still at that time. Laura even decided to stay overnight at my parents when I got released. Eventually, things started to settle down a bit, and Laura didn't come over every day anymore. She had her own things to take care of, after all. Boredom started to take over, which wasn't exactly a good sign.

I felt that I was being held captive again since I didn't have a way to see Laura. I argued with my parents till they allowed me to stay with her for the weekend at my place. I thought that things were going to return to normal again. Things were off between us and I was trying to get back on track with her emotions, but it wasn't happening.

However, Laura did not come over for Justin's birthday, which was very strange. It turns out she had moved out of our place and had blocked my number as well. She had reconnected with someone from her past while I was at the hospital, and she was now interested in him and wanted to cut things off with me. Laura is now married to him. I don't fault her for leaving.

Laura leaving me was very hurtful to me as I really liked her a lot and thought that we had a future. It was also an eye-opener of sorts since I went from seeing myself as Jesus Christ to being the guy that couldn't even keep his girlfriend. In the end, I don't blame her. I know I was a handful with my illusions of grandeur and my paranoia, and she probably just didn't want to deal with it anymore. I just wish she had been more open about it and had let me ease out of it beforehand and not just blocked me out the way that she did. Sometimes I think she would believe it all would return to normal too, which is why she quietly stood by my side for as long as she did. I should have thanked her for that, but how could I? My number was blocked. But well, it was what it was, and by August 2011, we were done.

Interestingly, the next time that I was in the same hospital as the one that separated Laura and me, I ended up finding another very interesting girl named Char. This was in May 2014, and I was hospitalized once again due to my grandiose behavior.

Char was a patient at the facility, just like I was. She was getting some help there too, and she seemed interested in me. We ended up rubbing each other while on the sofa and tried to sneak to places a couple of times. It was fun, and it helped me stay entertained while in the facility. When I got out, though, I told her that we were better off as friends. This was true since I wasn't very interested in her. She simply made the stay at the ward better. I think she took it well, and if she didn't, she never really showed any signs of it.

I haven't exactly dated anyone since. I've met a couple of girls, but that's about it. It's a temporary joy, but I haven't found someone to share my life with yet. But love has its ways of sneaking up on you when you least expect it, and it's not always evident. Who knows, maybe I've already met the girl that I'll marry and simply am not aware of it yet. Maybe Amanda will call me back, telling me how I have passed the test, and I can date Aimee now. I can only hope.

So there's my whole love life, right before you, and if you can't tell, it has been one roller coaster. It didn't exactly ever go smoothly, and I just had these ups and downs and ups and downs till it came to an end. At this point I'm not really dating anyone. But I think it wasn't without its lesson, and I learned a lot out of it.

I have grown to learn that love can be both toxic and overpowering. Too much of a good thing can kill you, or at least hurt you in other ways. It isn't always easy to understand and not always easy on you either. It can be like poison, slowly killing you, and it can overpower your other emotions and drive you to do things that you might not do otherwise. It's a lot like being drunk, like being under the influence. It's like someone else has taken the driver's seat and guides you through life and can leave you stranded wherever they want to and strand you. And I've found that to be true plenty of times like I did with Laura.

I think that I learned that love could be tough in my life, but it can also help you mature a lot. As I said, love is like poison, slowly killing you, but this gradual progress can make you immune to its toxic effects too. When I was young, love was very innocent and painless. It was simple crushes where I'd grow to like any girl that I thought was attractive and then try to get with her, and would often succeed. It didn't hurt when they left. I simply had to find another girl to obsess over. It was simple and plain and innocent.

It started to get worse into puberty to the point that it hurt, and I actually cried when Amanda left me, but I still didn't give too much thought to it. It was still simple, and I went for whoever I thought could be a fit for me and didn't think about if we'd be very compatible or not. It was still very much like childhood in a lot of ways.

Things started to change into adulthood. My relationships started to be more about what I wanted rather than getting whatever I could. I left Jackie and went for Missy since I knew that I had wanted Missy and not Jackie. I knew what would make me happy. I also knew that I had to play my part in keeping what made me happy with me. Instead of moving to just the choir as I did for Emily, I had to shift to an entirely different city for Missy's sake, but I still did. This was because I knew what my heart craved, and I knew how much I wanted her affection. The connection was so much deeper, and I could understand her.

This also meant that I could understand when she wanted to drift apart and couldn't keep up with me anymore due to her other obligations. The hurt was much more this time, almost to a profound extent, and I needed a distraction from it. I dated Teresa to help me overcome her because I knew that forgetting Missy was not going to be that simple. But I wasn't mad at Missy, and I understood that we hadn't worked out, and there was nothing that I could have done to change that given how she had no time to give to me. I guess when you love someone, it is easier to let them go, knowing that their life is theirs to live, and if it gets in the way, I have to do nothing except step aside.

My relationship with Laura was perhaps another eye-opener. I knew I wanted to be with her all the time, but she reconnected with someone else and rekindled an old flame. There's no going back from that, and I knew so. I wasn't going to try and argue my way into staying with her either. She had cut me off, and those were ties that you simply can't stick back with glue. Those ties, once cut, would not heal that easily. I knew and accepted that, and I moved on.

The next time I got even remotely close to dating was with Char, and this time I knew that this wasn't what I wanted right from the start. I didn't chase her because I thought she was the best I could get and needed someone. I simply told her the truth about how we were better off as friends.

I still get lonely. Especially when I have my episodes, it's not easy to get rid of the loneliness when you have no partner by your side to support you. But I think with time. I've learned to recognize that you can't love everyone, and you can't continue to be with someone you don't love or with someone who doesn't love you. Life has made me mature enough to cut off connections full of love if they ever get too toxic and empowering, and even though I'm all alone now, I think I'm on the right path, which will help me heal over time. As they say, the world was my oyster, and sometimes I felt like I was looking for a diamond in the rough instead of a pearl in the shell. Maybe I was looking in the wrong places? Who knows? All I knew is that I should not lose hope and let love come to me for once. Maybe this oyster of mine did make diamonds. Life can be surprising, more so when you think you have seen and done everything.

Chapter 8 – To Be 16 Again

In the Cadieux house is where my mother busted through my bedroom door and I managed to run to the door with my penis swinging and slammed the door back on her. She had just walked in on Missy and I having sex at age 15, on a bunk bed to top it off. It was the bottom bunk, if you must know. After we put our clothes on, we were going to have to face her. Her big, great plan was to send me to go talk to a priest and that kind of gave me a kick, because there are no words in the world that he could have relayed to me that would have stopped me from having sex with my beautiful girlfriend, sorry bro. I don't remember what was said, but it felt uncomfortable because he was the same priest, Fr. Burkart, that had baptized me as a baby.

In 1995, JavaScript, had just been released for the first time and Internet Explorer had just rolled out version 1.0. Only 14% of the world's population had access to the Internet and the US accounted for 9% of that. The top of the line modem had a speed of 28.8k and was connected to the phone line. My father was a computer programmer who spent half his time working from home and the other half of his time flying across the country helping to fix other people's coding issues. I was a sophomore in a high school with about 400 students and maybe around 30 of us had Internet access at home.

On one fateful day that summer of 95,' an America Online disk came in the mail with an offer of 90 free hours of Internet service. I did what any 15-year-old with access to a computer would do. I waited for my parents to go to sleep and then inserted the disk into my father's computer. The installation took forever! The modem was loud and made all kinds of screeching noises. I was afraid my parents would wake up and catch me, but they didn't. So I strapped on my seat belt and took a ride down the super information highway.

Many people thought AOL was the whole Internet and I'll even admit that I did too. When I had finished 'surfing' and it came time to go to sleep, I hid the AOL desktop icon with the idea that I could keep the install on the down-low from my father. It took him maybe a half hour the next day to discover what I had done and I was yelled at for the download. He told me it took up ALL his computer's memory and he couldn't perform his work-related tasks. The computer likely had 16 MB of RAM and a 500 MB hard drive. He uninstalled AOL and told me not to mess with his computer anymore. From that day forward, when I wasn't sneaking out, I had another night time routine.

Once my parents went to sleep, I'd download the AOL disk, surf the web for most of the night, and then uninstall the AOL program before dawn and catch a few hours of sleep before school. I was a midnight explorer of the web (well, of AOL, at least). There were so many bugs in Windows and AOL back then, you had to become a master of the task manager window to force programs to close. I was ahead of the curve by far at the time.

The big thing on the Internet, for males at least, was to exchange nude pictures. They were not nude selfies of yourself, but of other naked women. The Alicia Silverstone nude picture was the holy grail. Every celebrities' photo was just photo-shopped with their head put on somebody's body. I collected a lot of pictures and put them on to a floppy disk and stashed it with the rest of the disk filled with nudes. I'd delete the pictures off the computer and then I was in good shape. One would go into a chat room and ask if anybody wanted to trade pics. So, that's what I was doing when I wasn't out partying at the Wayburn and Novara houses. At least that's what 15 year old boys are doing. If you wanted to buy porn at the time you would go into a liquor store and they'd be behind the counter. I know somebody that did this a lot and spent a lot of money too. We had to work for our porn. We didn't just get it so easily and free as it comes today. Some friends would trade videos if theirs were growing stale. A new porno was almost as good as a new girlfriend.

Hank worked at a Kroger grocery store and that is where he met David. David was a cashier that became our good friend. He is the one that introduced us to Marsh's roommates, Mike, Matt, and James. David would hook them up with groceries. They would come in and fill up 2 or 3 baskets with food and when it came time to check out they would go down David's line. He would purposely skip over items so they wouldn't scan, but these guys were pushing the limit. They only had like $60 or something like that on (what should have been) a $300 bill. They always ate like kings for a few days after shopping. That was fun, because that's about the only time they weren't stingy.

We would go to the Wayburn house so we had somewhere to hang out other than Mesmer Park behind my house. They smoked our weed and we had a place to chill. They were about seven years older than us, so when we were 16, they were 23. We would go to their house on Wayburn pretty much daily. We used to buy our bags of pot from a guy named Kevin who lived in a trailer at Angel park, which wasn't too far from Wayburn, but then Kevin moved away and we had to find another place to score.

We were leaving the Wayburn house one day and a police car pulled up behind Dan's car, which was parked. There were four of us in the car. It was me, Hank, David, and Dan. The Grosse Pointe policeman walked up to our car and he said, "Hide the dope, hide the dope," as if he saw us shifting around in the car. The cops must have been watching the Wayburn house, but they didn't sell any drugs. They had zero dollars amongst them. The police man was pressuring us to give up the person that had the bag. I was the one holding the bag, I fessed up to him that it was my bag and I bought it somewhere other than the Wayburn house. He got me out of the car and I handed him the bag. He had me empty the quarter ounce down the sewer drain. It was great to get off easy for a change, but it hurt me to dump that bag though. They let us off with a warning, which in Grosse Pointe happens very rarely.

I had never met anybody like these fellas that lived there at the Wayburn house. Mike and Matt Ruby are twins; Mike went by Manix, Matt went by Butterfingers, James was Chaos Kid, and Marshall was m&m. We just called him Marsh though. One time I was over their house and stoned out of my mind. I looked in the fridge and grabbed the butter and searched for some bread. Matt was watching me like a hawk at the amount of butter I was spreading on the bread, and he made some remark like, "Not so much butter on that bread". These guys were arguing over butter. They were broke as hell. Mike and Matt did some house painting sometimes, but not very often and I don't remember James working either. Marsh worked at Gilbert's Lounge, which is a restaurant in St. Clair Shores just outside of Detroit.

Matt has a deformed hand and once you were stoned, he would put his hand in your face and ask you how many fingers he was holding up. There was never a correct answer, just awkwardness. He was fun to watch on the turn-tables though. That's why he was known as DJ Butterfingers. They had a little studio upstairs where my friends and I would watch them on the turn-tables and take turns rapping while drinking or smoking.

James Deel went by Chaos Kid. I really liked him. He was the nicest of the four, but sometimes he was just super goofy. James was renting the house on Wayburn from his uncle and they all stayed there. Marsh wasn't there that often, but he was at their next house on Novara a lot. He would usually be shooting baskets all damn day. James helped set up the show at Lakeview with Joe Joseph. Joe wanted to put on a show together so he helped organize it.

On weekends, Missy and I would spend most of our time hanging out with her friends from Grosse Pointe South High School. When we weren't partying at one of her rich friend's houses, we were either at Angel Park or at a motel near downtown Detroit called the Americana. Angel Park is a park in Detroit near Grosse Pointe off of Alter Road. Everybody would pull their cars into the parking lot and drink alcohol and socialize. It wasn't an ideal place to party because there was only one way in and out of the park. The police would come and bust us all the time. Mostly it was just taking our alcohol away, but the party always got broken up early.

The Americana motel was a run down, trashy motel that would allow us to party there. It was on Jefferson Ave. near downtown Detroit. It was the type of motel that charged by the hour, but it fit our purposes pretty well. It was a hooker and drug addict hangout, but that didn't stop us from having a good time there. One of Missy's friends made arrangements with the owner or manager and paid him a certain fee to let us party there and that's what we did.

Another of Missy's friends from school, named Costa owned a Coney Island restaurant. He would throw awesome parties there when it was closed for business. People would come in and party and he would also sell us alcohol. He made out pretty good for himself for sure.

We threw Justin a surprise party for his 19th birthday at our house on Cadieux and we had a couple of kegs to celebrate. Now that Justin was 19, I was essentially 19 years old too, because we looked similar and I was able to use his ID. That doesn't mean much in the US, but

Windsor, Ontario, Canada is just a short drive through the tunnel or over the bridge in Detroit and the drinking age is 19. Justin and I would go there with one of my employees from Jets named Anthony and his friend Choo Choo. Bentleys was the most popular bar and it was pretty cool to be there at age 16. The beer in Canada is stronger than it is in the US, so it was easier to catch a buzz and at the time the currency exchange rate was pretty good, like .70 US to $1 CAN.

Chapter 9 – 1997

In November of my junior year, I took a Saturday night off from work to go to a Green Day concert with Missy and another couple. Ken was a senior at my school and I also gave him a delivering job at Jets. He and his girlfriend came with us to the concert. Derrick, the owner filled in for me for the night. We did some pre-drinking before the concert and had a really good time. After the concert, I had decided to bring them all back to Jets to make some pizzas.

We were in there long enough to turn the ovens back on and put some pizzas in the oven, when the Grosse Pointe Police began knocking on the door. I tried explaining to them that I was the manager and had every right to be in there. Apparently, Derrick had driven one of the employees home after the shift and had seen us while passing back by. He didn't know who we were so he called the cops. When he arrived and saw that I had turned the ovens back on and had pizza in the oven, he fired me on the spot and asked me for the keys back. It was pretty embarrassing. I was showing off and got canned by the owner. It was a devastating blow to my ego.

I was unemployed for a few months until I found a job and started working at Mamma Rosa's Pizzeria. Instead of managing however, I was managing the production of dough for the pizzas. Whereas at Jet's we were making 5 to 6 batches of dough tops; at Mamma Rosa's we were making an average of 10 batches of dough per weekend night. I was in charge of the dough and I had two helpers with me that would help roll the dough into balls and later stretch them into pans. I was great at my job, but the pay was peanuts compared to what I was used to.

Mama Rosas was just a couple of blocks away from the Wayburn house, but the guys from Wayburn had already moved to the Novara house by then. I worked there mostly on the weekends and I would try to complete my work as fast as I could and leave them prepared so I could leave as early as possible and hang out with Missy. The owner, Tony, had a little office in the back of the place and he would have friends come in to hang out with him. I found myself in that office on numerous occasions to get pay advances on my check and Tony was real cool about that. Sometimes on payday he would throw me a little extra, like a $20 to keep me happy. He knew I was a really good worker.

In January of 1997, my brother Scott had a surprise going away party thrown for him at the other Scott's house on E. Outer Drive. My brother had graduated from the University o Michigan and was moving away to Portland, Oregon to start a new job. It was a fairly small gathering, but what stood out to me, was that I overheard my father saying to Scott's friends, "One out of three ain't bad". Meaning one successful kid out of three wasn't bad. That fact that I still remember him saying that must mean something about our relationship.

My mother had run for the position of Pension Trustee for the City of Detroit and although it was a long shot that she would win, being a white female, she mustered up the votes to pull off the win. Her and a board of 9 other trustees were in charge of investing the pension money for the employees of the city of Detroit. This fund had a couple billion dollars in it. With her position came the perk of traveling all over the world to conferences and other opportunities that involved investing the city's pension fund. On some occasions she was able to bring me or other family members with her.

On March 8, 1997, my grandmother, Jean Wojcik, my mother's mother, died. She lived out her final years in nursing homes after we moved her out of our house due to needing around the clock care. We picked her up to celebrate most holidays and the ones we couldn't, we would bring the celebration to her at the nursing home. She lived another 40 years after her husband Edward Wojcik died of a heart attack while shoveling the snow.

Missy's group of friends from Grosse Pointe South were planning a spring break trip to Cancun, Mexico and she formulated a plan that would allow me to go too. I would give her money from my paycheck every week and she would hold onto it for me so I wouldn't spend it on stupid shit like beer and weed. I wasn't really making much money at all at the time, so I was no longer balling like I was when I worked at Jets.

In the end of March, I went on spring break with Missy and her group of friends and returned in the beginning of April. We stayed at the Oasis Resort and had all inclusive drinks that came with our package through a travel agent. I'm pretty sure I was the only one in the group that saved my own money for the trip. My parents did end up giving me some spending money though. Most of us were still 17 years old and hadn't turned 18 yet, but it didn't matter there. The drinking age may have been 16 years old there, but nobody really cared at the clubs or resort regardless.

My mother had the opportunity to go to South America for one of the pension fund conferences and she had discussed me going on the trip with my principal at Notre Dame High, Mr. Richard Kuhn. He agreed with my mother that it would be a great experience for me, so he allowed me to miss school to go. The trip would be two weeks after I returned home from my spring break trip to Cancun, Mexico.

As soon as we were to return from Cancun, I was to spend a week at school and then leave for the trip to South America with my mother. On the flight home from Cancun, I felt unbelievable sick. I had drank the night before we left, so I thought I was just hungover. We had a layover in Houston, Texas and as soon as I got off the first plane I threw up in the nearest garbage can. My head was pounding too, but again I just thought it was a hangover. They tell you not to drink the water in Mexico or else you will get Montezuma's Revenge, which is basically diarrhea and other flu like symptoms.

We were very careful about drinking bottled water while we were in Cancun, but there's just some nights when you're drunk and you are out of bottled water in the room and you take a drink from the faucet. That's most likely what I did anyhow. It may have been from ice cubes or something similar, but the fact of the matter is that's what I got. So, when I got home from the trip, I was laid up in bed for a whole week. I missed the week of school between my vacations. I thought I was going to be buried with homework when I finally did come back to school.

It was my first international flight from Detroit to Santiago, Chile and it was super strange back in the day. On this flight, they had a smoking section, which was like the last three rows on the plane. My mother and I both smoked, so it was excellent for us, but I can't imagine being those people in the row fourth and fifth from the back. Having smoke being blown over your shoulder while you're on a plane doesn't seem too appealing, but it worked out great for us! If you're a non-smoker, which I have been before, It would make me nauseous to be in a big tube in the sky filled with smoke from a bunch of people lighting up.

Everything that we did in South America was first-class and larger than life. We stayed at the nicest hotel money could buy and dined at the most exquisite restaurants where the wine never stopped flowing. You could take 3 or 4 sips from your wine glass and the waiter would be right over your shoulder to top your glass off. Pension vendors are companies that want to be the ones to invest your pension funds, so they can make a fee.

They always went out of their way to spend loads of money to butter up the trustees.

There were conferences during the day where they would have important people like the Vice President of Chile talking about currencies and why you should invest your money in their economy and many other big whigs that spoke on various financial and economic topics. Pension funds are so large, almost always in the billions of dollars, that everybody is trying to get a piece of the pie. Say somebody works for the city of Detroit for 30 years and paid into their pension. It's up to the pension board of trustees to find smart people and make wise investments with that money. They have to be able to pay these former employees until they die.

Now, just because these vendors were spending a ton of money entertaining the trustees, doesn't mean they will get their vote to invest the pension fund. They have to back that jazz up with solid numbers and proof of past successes. The vendors want a good relationship with the trustees, because they think it may help them get a deal in the future with the pension fund, but it doesn't always work out that way. They may be able to convince a few of the trustees to let the vendors be heard at a board meeting to present a deal, but it didn't guarantee a favorable vote.

When I say vendors, I'm talking about banks and investment firms. They have the sociable guys go out and schmooze the trustees and it's all company write-offs for them. The vendors all pitch in and rent the nicest hotel in the city with a conference hall there with great lunches served. When it's time to take in the city, the vendors will pay for tour guides and all that hoopla. Dinners were the best though. Five star restaurants serving the best steaks and seafood with a never ending drink in your hand.

On one occasion a few of the vendors rented out a ranch called the Gaucho. They paid for a tour bus to take us an hour out of the city of Santiago where they had horses and cowboys and you just got that ranch feeling.

Chile is known for their beef and their wine. At the Gaucho Ranch, they were cooking all kinds of beef on the grill and it was a real site. Until a little later when my mother and I noticed the huge amount of flies sitting on some of the meat they had cooked. As I recalled that was pretty much an appetite ruiner for us.

During one of our outings my mother and I stopped at a mall in Santiago. It was an outdoor mall and it was amazing. They had all the same shops that we have in the States. I didn't really know what to expect when I heard I was going to Santiago, Chile. I was 17 years old and I think I was expecting to see huts or something. They had nicer malls than I had ever been to in Detroit. I grew up going to Eastland Mall on 8 Mile where they had shootings happening and crappy stores.

Lastly, they brought us to the Chilean Stock Exchange during open hours and we were able to watch the stock brokers buying and selling stocks. It was a cool site. It's just like when you watch a movie with everyone yelling in the NY Stock Exchange, but these guys were talking in Spanish. That wrapped up our trip in Santiago, Chile and then we were off to Argentina.

Of the two countries, I liked Argentina much more and I had a lot more fun there. We went to Buenos Aires and stayed in the nicest hotel in that city too. It was the same one Madonna stayed at when she was filming the movie Evita about the First Lady of Argentina from 1946 until her death in 1952. The Presidential Palace in Argentina is known as the Pink House instead of our White House.

We visited a cemetery that contained Evita Perone's mausoleum along with many other famous Argentinians. Mausoleums are buildings, especially large and stately ones, housing a tomb or tombs. We saw some that contained husband and wife together and even whole families. You could tell who was the most rich by how big their mausoleums were.

We did the same types of fine dining in Buenos Aires as we did in Santiago, Chile. What made Buenos Aires more fun for me is that I was hanging out with a group of people who were more fun. I met this guy named Tim Holt from Wisconsin and we had an immediate connection. I don't know if he was just trying to get my mom's vote, but I don't think he was. He was a Vice President of some bank and we had a good time and a lot of laughs together.

On the last night following dinner, we continued the party back at our hotel's lobby bar and had some more drinks and once my mother had had enough, she went up to the hotel room. Tim and a couple other vendors brought me across the street to this bar called the Black Piano. It was an upstairs bar, so you had to get past the bouncer on the bottom stairwell and walk up some stairs to get up to the bar. There was no cover charge, which I found odd, because most clubs we had gone to had them. When I walked in all I saw were beautiful women. There were hardly any guys there at all and when we went to the bar to get drinks, I learned that each beer costed $25. I knew I wasn't paying, so I wasn't worried, but I began to wonder what was going on and then it dawned on me. We were in a hooker bar and the women were lined up and beautiful.

We got our beers and drinks and grabbed a table and started to look around. Tim and the other guys knew exactly where we were, but I was still trying to figure the situation out. The woman would come to your table and flirt and ask you to buy them a $25 to $40 drink and they would provide you with company at your table. The bar was making money from expensive drinks and the woman would basically try and garner interest in themselves so that you would take them back to your hotel room with you. That's where the money was made, but these weren't some cheap hookers. They were young and beautiful.

It was like being at the opposite of a regular club anywhere. Women were vying for your attention not only to get you to buy them some drinks for the house, but the women were actually hitting on you. It wasn't a strip club. The woman were dressed as if they were at any other club, but they were all prostitutes. Rumor has it that many highly influential people in Argentina frequented that place and I could tell why. After spending a few hours there and probably close to a thousand dollars, we stumbled back across the street to our hotel rooms. Some of the guys had a woman with them, but I left empty handed. I didn't have the money or my own hotel room although I contemplated playfully bringing one into the bathroom at our hotel room while my mother slept. Plus, I had Missy back home waiting for me and I would see her in a day or two anyway.

My father picked my mother and me up from the airport and asked about out trip and we gave him the rundown. But when we were finished, he told me that he had some bad news for me. He told me my friend Brian Barrett from grade school sports and high school had committed suicide on April 11, 1997, just 5 weeks from graduation. I was stunned. I was jealous of this kid for the last 6 or 7 years of my life and he killed himself. My grade school crush dated him, he was an excellent athlete, and women adored him. We carpooled to school together everyday freshman year and often took the bus home from school together too. He had died a day or two after I left on my trip, but my father didn't want to inform me over the phone while I was out of town.

I have had the opportunity to travel a lot in my life. Teresa and I went to Amsterdam, Belgium, and France back in 2001. Because of my mother's position, I was able to go on the South American trip and she also took me to Ireland. I've been to many of the States in the U.S. and spent extensive time in LA, Austin, and Florida. It's really nice to get away from Detroit and if you live here, you know why. It's like there's a dark cloud that hovers over Detroit that's not there when you go other places. Other people are proud to live where they live and it's not like that for most people from Detroit. Many are just a victim of circumstance, while others have mental barriers that stop them from leaving. Don't get me wrong, I'm proud to have grown up in Detroit, but that doesn't mean I want to live here my entire life. It can be depressing here with the long winters and the level of poverty.

Chapter 10 – College Life

Since this book took me five years from conception to production, I've written it in different phases of my life. When I first started writing, I was having my second or third manic episode and I felt that I should write my story down. I sat at a desk in my bedroom and wrote the first 40 pages in one sitting. Of course that version has been edited, but it laid the groundwork for what was to become this book. I had an idea for a book and perhaps a screenplay called Hate/Smile back in 2016 and I posted it to Facebook. Yes, it was another manic idea that ended up sticking in the end. I like Hate/Smile because it rhymes with 8 Mile. I went to school on 8 Mile and I used to hang out with Eminem and the crew at 7.5 Mile and Kelly. Plus, you have the movie and song by Eminem.

The Greatest Story Never Told also came from a manic episode. I was originally going to call it the Greatest Story Ever Told, but somebody on Facebook told me that was what they called the Bible, so I decided they could keep it and I would change mine. Plus, if I never actually finished the book, I could just chalk it up to a manic episode I had once had and Never actually told the story. Thus, The Greatest Story Never Told. I think I have a great story and I'm hoping you do too. I'm really trying my best to overdeliver, because I've been underwhelmed myself by many books.

If I had finished my book back in 2016 or 2017 even, I wouldn't have had half the content that was provided in the last 5 years. That's everything from my police beatdown in Austin to my cross country arrest spree where I went to jail in Florida, Georgia, and Michigan all during one manic episode. When I got the beatdown I had already started the book, so I knew, somewhat, what I was doing, but it cost me much more than I ever imagined. Two and a half years without a license and probation for 5 years.

I want to summarize some of my life for you quickly, so that you and I are on the same page. I grew up in Detroit and had a group of friends from childhood through high school. My oldest friends were Dan Minor, Hank, Hank's little brother Reggie, and Ryan. I had other friends from sports and school, but those were my homies. I dated a few girls throughout middle school and junior high, but my first serious relationship was with Missy. I stabbed Hank in the back and ended up with Missy as my girlfriend my sophomore year of high school. We dated for three and a half years and eventually broke up to 'see other people'. That is, until she found a boyfriend. All of a sudden I was the odd man out and it was her cheating on him with me!

Next came Teresa when I was 19 years old. I don't discuss Teresa much in this book, but she does appear in my next book. We dated for 7 long and crazy years and eventually went our separate ways when she moved to Florida. When I was with Teresa, I lived in Ypsilanti to begin with and then later moved in with her. We lived together for a couple years and then decided to each move back to our parent's house. Pretty odd, eh? The relationship was never moving forward. We took many steps back, but never discussed the future together.

I spent too much time working at Fishbones and hanging out with Teresa and my workmates and not enough time studying for school. I was doing very poorly in my classes my sophomore year in college. I eventually stopped going to class, but didn't have the foresight to withdraw from the classes, so I got F's. I flunked out of school and cost my parents $50,000 along the way. I was making killer money waiting tables at Fishbones though. Sometimes up to $250 per shift and usually a guaranteed $100

When Teresa and I decided to move back with our parents there was a reason for me to. My mother offered to send me to Macomb Community College, but only if I lived under her roof. This really irritated me and I felt like she was being controlling. But the fact of the matter is that she wanted to keep an eye on her investment. Last time she had spent $50k for me to piss away at University and she wanted to make sure I didn't do it again. I studied General Business at Community College and managed to get my Associates Degree with honors. I actually had 4.0 semesters, which didn't exactly surprise me. I knew if I applied myself I could do well in school and that's just what I did. I'd wait until all of my homework was done before I would spark up a joint as a reward. Whatever works, right?

Since, I didn't have anybody going away to school with me, I was assigned a roommate for the dorm room. My roommate Pat and I got along pretty well. He was the guy that would kind of make fun of me for being a stoner and I would poke fun at him that he was still a virgin. He bought a 100 disc CD changer with some big ass speakers and loaded up all of his CD's into it. I had brought one CD from home with me and it was Sublime's 1996 album. Pat would put his CD player on random and Sublime's "What I Got" would come on more than any other of his music and it would drive him mad! He would get so pissed off. It was great to watch him get frustrated.

Close to the end of the first semester, Missy and I were still going strong and I had met a few friends. Josh, lived directly across the hall from me and Jim lived two doors down. The three of us liked to party a lot. I had my brother Justin's ID still, so when I went away to college at 18, I could buy alcohol with his ID that said I was 21. This was a blessing and a curse, because on the one hand I could buy alcohol, on the other hand, Josh would bother me almost daily to go to the store for him to buy a couple 40 ounce beers. I had it well, because I could go to the bars if I wanted, but my friends couldn't get in.

Josh was a character like I had never met before. He had so many photos of him from back home and growing up as a teenager, it kind of made me envious. He liked showing them to you to and behind every photo there was a story and Josh was happily ready to tell you it. After a while, you were just like, come on man. I just want to enjoy my buzz. He was a writer too, so you had to listen to him read his writings to you and his writings were good, but they were deep. Deeper than I can go honestly and it'd be the same thing; you're ruining my buzz. He and I spent a lot of time together drinking and smoking.

Jim was a year older than Josh and I and he was more heavily into hip hop than Josh and I were at the time. I guess you can call Bone Thugs' n Harmony hip hop at least. He liked to dress more hip hop than us at least. He dated a real cute blonde haired, blue eyed girl named Kim and the two of them spent a lot of time together, so Josh and I were a little bit closer than Jim and I. He, his roommate Steve, and I used to play a lot of Tecmo Bowl football on Super Nintendo and we started getting into gambling against each other. Jim was a big gambler and he would make his way over to Windsor Casino with Kim on some weekends. I went with them once and watched Kim win $700 on a slot machine.

Pat would get pissy if we smoked weed in our dorm room so I usually ended up at one of their rooms to smoke. We had a resident advisor named Milo that lived on our floor and was in charge of enforcing the rules. He was a muscular, black guy from Detroit and he was real cool. Josh and I were smoking in his room one time and he smelled the weed so he started banging on Josh's door. We were terrified. We didn't answer the door and just hoped he's go away and he finally did. We were paranoid as fuck that he was going to call the police, but that didn't happen. Out of all the weed we smoked in those dorm rooms, that was the only close call we had we had with Milo.

Our dorms were across the street from an old dilapidated paper factory and the three of us would walk over there sometimes to smoke. It was right on the Huron River and there was a park called Peninsular Park. The paper mill was right on the river and there was a waterfall that was probably useful to them at some point We had to climb a fence to go stand near it, while we smoked. I'd bring Missy there a few times when she came to visit. It was so cool. For us, it provided us something to do to get out of the dorms and drink or smoke some weed.

Josh wasn't a good student that first semester, because he was always drinking and he worked at Outback Steakhouse and knew some other people he was hanging around. He went on a trip to Austin, Texas on winter break and landed himself in jail for a few days for minor in possession or something like that. When he returned to school, I had never seen someone so focused before in my life. Now, he would only party once his school work was done and not put it off, like Jim and I began to do.

My mother had a friend that ran some parking lots in Ann Arbor and was able to get me a weekend gig when University of Michigan had home football games. I would stand in a parking lot and only let people in that had parking passes and when it got close to game time, if there was still space available, I could let some cars in for $20 a pop. It was hard waking up on those Saturdays at 7am in the morning, but I made $60 for a few hours of work and I needed the money, so that's what I did. It was exhilarating watching the U of M students pregame, party in the parking lots, and then make their way walking down the streets for the games. The stadium holds around 105,000 people.

I had to be on the lot at 8am for games that started at noon or 1pm and there was a parking lot right next to mine that threw excellent pregame parties. They often fed me some of their really good food too, so that was cool. It got interesting when the lot was almost full and I had cars with rich alumni pulling up and offering me $60-$120 for a parking space. I would pretty much fit them in no matter how full the lot was at that point. Sometimes I made some extra money that way because it was considered a tip in my book.

On November 22, of 1997 Missy and I went to the University of Michigan football game against Ohio State. She was a season ticket holder and was able to doctor her receipt ticket to look like another ticket, so I could get in too. It worked because there's so many people coming into the game, the people at the gate just glance at it and let you walk by. I'm sure they have barcode scanners today, so that would never work, but it did back in 1997. The University of Michigan team was playing in week 11 and they were going for a perfect season against their rival Ohio State.

Up to that point, the stadium had never held 107,000 people so it was a record breaking attendance. If they had accounted for the people with the fake tickets, like I had, who knows how many people were packed into Michigan Stadium. There were people standing in the rows of stairs all throughout the place. Once the game had ended and Michigan beat Ohio State 20-14, people began to rush onto the field. The first crowd of people were sprayed with tear gas, but that didn't deter more people from rushing the field. The security just gave up and stopped tear gassing people, so we made our way onto the field too. I even dug up some grass from the field and later put it into a plastic bag.

Eastern Michigan became a relative ghost town on the weekends and it wasn't the party I had expected. During that second semester throughout 1998, I noticed the students in my dorm would go home to their family and friends almost every weekend. I didn't have a car because my Volkswagen had gotten totaled the previous year, so I wasn't at liberty to go very far. The weekend visits with Missy became more rare as she had studying to do or she would be attending social events with her sorority. Josh was working at Outback Steakhouse on the weekends and Jim was normally hanging out with Kim somewhere.

I struggled my first bout of depression at that time. I would roam the hallways of my dorm just kind of looking for something to do. It became more difficult to focus on studying the way I was throughout the first semester. I didn't seriously consider suicide, but there were times I looked out the window of my 4th floor dorm room and thought what if as if that were an option. Missy and I had considered seeing other people and it was eating away at me. I was the kind of guy you got to know slowly and you figured out that you liked. I had walls built up that just didn't allow me to go up to people and spill my heart out. I didn't make friends easily and I wasn't exactly great at courting women. Whereas Missy probably had a line of guys waiting to date her, I would have to try real hard to procure another woman.

School was out for the summer in May, so Missy and I had come back to Detroit and stayed with our families. On the morning of May 8, 1998, I was sleeping in my room at my parent's house and was awakened by Justin. He told me that my best friend Hanks' brother Reggie had committed suicide. The kid I had known since first grade. I was in shock. I thought to myself, "Not again. This is the second time in a year" but this time it hit even closer to home. Reggie wasn't just my best friend's brother, he was a close friend of mine too.

Reggie was always coming up with money to buy weed and other things and we could never figure out how. He told us that sometimes he would go out with some of his thug friends and steal speakers and amplifiers out of people's trunks of their cars. It was feasible that he had been doing that sometimes, but it didn't really account for the money he was able to spend. He worked at Buddy's pizza a few shifts per week, but still, that didn't account for the money either.

It turns out that Reggie was stealing jewelry from his mother and having our friend Ryan pawn it at the pawnshops on Gratiot Avenue. Ryan didn't know it was Reggie's mother's stuff he was pawning, but I'm sure he knew there was something sinister about Reggie always having this jewelry to pawn. Reggie was a little shady, but he was Hank's little brother I had grown up with and he never fucked with me or my stuff, so we were cool in that department.

Hank and Reggie's mom, Daad, starting calling the parents of their friends to see if anybody knew about her jewelry that had come up missing. Sure enough, Dan's parents happened to be driving down Gratiot Avenue one day when they saw Reggie and Ryan leaving a pawn shop, so Dan's mother relayed this information to their mom, Daad. When Reggie came home that night, she laid into him pretty good, just like anybody's mother would have done. I don't know what she said that may or may not have crossed the line for him, but he went to sleep that night with the intention of killing himself the next morning.

On the morning of May 8, Reggie's father also named Reginald woke him up for school and told him he'd be waiting in the car to drive him. Reggie said, "I'll be right with you". Reggie went down to the basement of their house and used a shotgun to shoot himself in the head. I guess he was so guilt ridden by what he had done to his mother, he couldn't go on living anymore.

Shortly after I had woken up and heard the news, Dan and Ryan came over to our house and we all were in shock talking about what had happened.   Ryan was devastated and thought we were accusing him in taking part in the theft of the jewelry. Unbeknownst to him, he was the one pawning the jewelry, because he was 18 and Reggie was 17. He committed suicide 5 weeks before his

18th birthday. Back then, we placed some of the blame on Dan's mother for ratting them out about seeing them at the pawnshop, but that's what almost any mother would have done in that situation.

I went to Hank's house to comfort him and to see if there was anything I could do to help. His father said, "Neal, you better not be on those drugs too!". I guess his parents wanted to blame his death on using marijuana. Hank had told me that he was responsible for cleaning up all of the blood that was on the basement floor. He also had to call his family members and notify them of Reggie's death and upcoming funeral arrangements. Pretty hefty task for a 19 year old if you ask me, but his mother, Daad, could not be consoled and was just grief stricken as you can imagine. It was a no win situation for her. What was she not supposed to chastise her son for stealing from her? She wanted to place the blame elsewhere, like on his friends and the use of weed.

Turning to Missy for consolence was of no help at this time either. She knew Reggie pretty well too, but she had made plans to go back up to Ann Arbor for a party that weekend. I couldn't believe she was going to just leave me and go party at U of M. I had stormed out of her house when I learned she still planned on going and took off in my car. She eventually did end up staying back in Detroit, but later told me she had begun to see someone else while away at school. She told me the day my friend had killed himself, so that didn't help matters any. She should have just went and partied.

After a long day, I came home and felt compelled to write about the events of the day and where my mind was at. I wrote a few pages on Microsoft Windows and saved the document thinking I would want it someday. I wish I had that now, but my sister in-law threw away my hard drive that had all of my important documents on it, because she found my porn stash.

The funeral for Reggie was depressing as could be. All of his classmates, close friends, and relatives were there and his mother was wailing and wailing in grief. It was quite disturbing and caused an emotional scene. Hank was strong as one could be and he was the rock for his mother and father. His mother disliked me, because whenever Hank would get caught with something like weed or cigarettes, he'd blame it on me. I guess he didn't think very far ahead, because that just made her dislike me in the long run. He was just thinking about how to get out of trouble at the moment. She was nice to me at the funeral though. I had sat on her lap and read to her when I was 7 years old and knew them for 12 years.

A week after Reggie's funeral, my parents and I had a trip planned to go to San Diego, California for my cousin Stacy's wedding. We flew to San Diego and were able to catch up with my aunt Jan, uncle Pete, and cousins Stacy and Donavon before the wedding took place. My cousin Stacy was marrying someone she had been dating for a long time named Sean. They took me out to a few San Diego bars a couple days before the wedding and showed me the California way to drink a beer, which was to add lime to it. I was 19 and since I was with them nobody carded me since they were regulars there. It wouldn't have mattered anyway, because I was still using Justin's ID religiously.

It was a huge wedding and there were a lot of people I had never met before, but since they were friends of Stacy's and Sean's, they were all good people. I drank a lot at the wedding and after the reception went back to the motel room with my parents. I really wanted to see my old neighborhood in Spring Valley where I lived when I was 10, so I waited for my parents to fall asleep and took the rental car for a ride. I cruised around for a bit, until I was able to find my direction and somehow I was able to navigate my way to my old neighborhood. They didn't have navigation systems in the cars and there were no smartphones, so I'm even surprised I was able to find it. I did however, and took a trip down memory lane. I even found my way back to the motel when I was finished.

On our way home to Detroit after the wedding we had plans to meet my brother, Scott, in Las Vegas for a couple days. We played blackjack in the casinos and I had a good old time. Scott was 24 at the time and I was 19 using Justin's ID again to get into the casinos and gamble and drink. There were a couple of times when my mom, Scott, and I were sitting at the same table winning money. Vegas offered free drinks and cigarettes to people gambling, so that made it even more fun. During the day we would sit by the pool at our hotel and towards night time we would either gamble in our casino or hit the strip and try our luck at one of the smaller casinos. Overall, I broke about even, but the free drinks and smokes made up for any loses I may have incurred.

I had brought a little one hitter dugout with me, so I would sneak away from my family and hit on that when I could. Just about every time I traveled by plane I would manage to bring some weed with me. Whether I put it in my underwear or in my checked in luggage, I never had a problem. I had heard that in Las Vegas they were real strict with weed, so I would go to the pool late at night when nobody was around and sneak hits from my one hitter. I didn't smoke much during the day, because I was paranoid of the cops busting me, plus I was already drinking nonstop. It felt pretty cool being 19 in Vegas and still being able to partake in the gambling and drinking.

Missy and I had pretty much called it quits around this point in time even though we went through the motions like most breakups do and that was still seeing each other sparingly until the feeling drifted away. I spent the summer living with my parents on Cadieux in Detroit and she lived with her parents in Grosse Pointe, but she would head back up to Ann Arbor a lot of the weekends. She had her sorority up there and the new guy she was seeing.

Hank needed to get away from Detroit and his parents after Reggie's death, so him and I got a place in Ypsilanti. He didn't go to Eastern, but was able to transfer to a Kroger grocery store in Ann Arbor, which was close by. He and I lived together and later when Josh needed a place to stay, he moved in too. Never become roommates with your close friends! Hank and I had a hard time getting along for a while when I lived there. For one, he liked to talk shit about me behind my back. I think this was partially because I stole his girlfriend and deserved it and partially out of jealousy, I guess.

Ok, back on track now. After Teresa there was Laura, whom I met on the dating website Match.com. Those were the relationships in my life. Three and a half years with Missy, seven years with Teresa, and another three and a half years with Laura. We won't count Char, because we shouldn't.

After I got my associates degree from Macomb Community College, I started pursuing my bachelor's degree at Oakland University. I would do stupid shit like take a difficult math class along with 3 other classes, one of them being Japanese. I kept failing the pre-calculus class that was required for my degree, so I looked for another option.

I was offered a full ride scholarship to Baker College, which was kind of crazy. I know I had done well in Community College, but I didn't expect any kind of scholarship. It turns out they were trying to get their graduate ratio up, so they would offer older students like me a free ride. It helped boost their numbers and everybody was happy. Except me, of course. Now, I have a degree from a no name college and haven't used it in any form or capacity since I've graduated. The admissions lady lied to me and told me I wouldn't have to take any more math classes, but lucky for me it was just Algebra and a Business Math course.

Chapter 11 - Being Bipolar is no Walk in the Park, I Tell You

Perhaps, one of the most recurrent themes of this book is my bipolar disorder, which has haunted me for the past decade of my life and made things difficult for me. Bipolar disorder is one of those things that can be difficult to determine if you are not the one experiencing it. I know this because of how everyone acted when I was having one of my episodes. Through this chapter, I will attempt to help you understand it better and tell you more about the episodes and what went on in my head during them, and how I felt.

If I have to give a simplistic, yet holistic definition, I would say that being bipolar is like experiencing highs and lows, but to a severe extreme. The highs are extremes, the kind that make you feel invincible, able to conquer the world singlehandedly, and the lows take you to places deep below, farther than the light can ever go, where you see nothing but darkness. It skews your sense of self, and there is nothing but blackness in every direction, and you cannot even see your shadow. Your brain effectively takes note of nothing except that enigma, and like a bottomless hole, you fall, and you keep falling deep beneath. There is a reason that bipolar disorder used to be called manic depression. The manic is the high, and the depression is the low, and they could not be farther from each other. What makes bipolar disorder such a severe condition is that it is not just chronic, but lifelong. You are stuck with it, and an episode can occur at anytime, in any number of intervals. In some cases, it can even lead to psychosis, where your conscious can experience a sudden break from reality, a rift from what is real into a place that only their psychotic selves can describe.

The first episode happened when I was with Laura at the festival. I know you have already heard about this, and I promise that this is not another one of my moments when I think I am above it all. This time, it won't be a recollection of the event, but rather, how I felt as it happened. In all those moments, what I felt mattered the most because it dictated what I did. If I felt like I was on top of the world, I began looking down at everyone. I felt like nothing would ever go right, well, you can imagine.

I was very paranoid at that time. You see, I began growing and selling medical marijuana. It was good money. I had more cash on hand than ever before. Things were going good, too good, and doubt began to set it. I imagined – no, knew – that I was being watched by someone, anyone, for the weed I sold. I was jumpy, looking over my shoulder at every sound, trying to look as inconspicuous as possible when I went out in public. When you are paranoid, every normal little thing becomes yet another way you can be caught, another way 'they' can get you. When we were going to enter the festival, we were asked to show our IDs. Of course, if I weren't being paranoid at that time, I would think nothing of it, and nothing would happen. Asking for your IDs is a normal process. We are all used to it. We do not question it. I outright refused because I thought he was trying to catch me and put me in jail. We argued back and forth till he eventually gave in and let us pass. I was also feeling grandiose, on top of the world, so I paid for everything on the trip with the $1200 I had gotten by selling the weed.

When we went around to putting the tent up, it proved to be far more difficult than it should have been. I had put up tents before. Doing it again should not have been a big deal, but unlike before, I was on another type of high. I was thinking of myself as flawless, someone epic. I was feeling grandiose. You can imagine what it can do. It is like a professional footballer not being able to score from a dead ball or a shooter failing to hit a target at point-blank range. As one might expect, I got frustrated, and I was a complete jerk to both Laura and Justin. I even berated a woman that offered to help us. After quite a bit of argument, we finally figured out that we were missing a few pieces. We ended up getting a new one from Walmart. That did not help my already difficult behavior.

Then we went up to the festival, and I looked up at the stage, and in a moment of madness, asked Laura if I should get up there. Her refusal really hurt. I did not think I was being unreasonable in the slightest. In fact, I thought that I was allowing her great honor. Being commanded up to the stage by someone like me would be the dream of anyone, and I did not expect her even to hesitate, much less refuse outright. I was already agitated by the incident with the tent. This just made it worse. Couple that with some paranoia, and you have a recipe for chaos. I didn't know what I was going to say once I was on stage though. 'Everybody bow down to me". It was very livid, and my grandiose behavior was clearly expressing itself more and more. With every passing moment, I was getting worse, expecting more and more people to adhere to my commands, to bow before me in awe of my presence.

By this point, Laura and Justin had noticed something was wrong and convinced me to go home. Things didn't get any better on the way, though. I was convinced that a car was trying to follow us when it was simply going down the road. Every time a car passed us, I thought that it was just a ploy to get my guard down. Every time a car would be behind us, I knew I was being followed. I also tapped on the roof, thinking that I was signaling to a satellite in space. Was it in Morse code? Or had I suddenly invented a new type of communication where a satellite would be able to pick up knocking sounds in the car? Making sense of the situation did not matter to me. I did not consider the fact that it was possible for me to be wrong. I was trying to decode messages in license plates and signs as we drove home. I had read a story about using Cipher keys to decode messages, and while I did not know what I used, I managed to decode the plate on a Pinto that said 'Hi43,' or 'hide.' Needless to say, Laura and Justin were spooked. When I tried to convince them that the car behind us will try to catch us, they exchanged knowing looks between each other.

When we got home, I pulled the most grandiose trick of all. I wanted to get one over everything I had done that night. I wanted to out-do myself. I wanted to be recognized for who I really was. I went and grabbed the prayer cards from my Grandparents' funeral, laid them down, and started chanting "Matthew, Mark, Luke, and John" over and over again. I thought that I was Jesus Christ and I was going to reveal some great mystery. I was telling my parents that I was able to 'Connect the dots". Thinking of yourself as some sort of king that everyone should bow down to is one thing, but to reach divinity is a different kind of danger. It is not that I thought I could not do wrong. It is that I thought I could only ever do right. There was no notion of doing something I should not have, as everything I did had a reason. My reason. I was now Jesus Christ. It did not matter what I did because everything I did mattered.

Later that night, I went out of my room and ran onto the street in my underwear. I just thought of it as this new fashion trend that I started and that everyone else would quickly follow suit. Everyone looked up to me, so why would they not follow in my footsteps. Well, my dad did not think so. He followed me in a car and tried to coax me back home, but I shouted at him and refused. It continued for a while. My dad would try to convince me one way or another to get back home, but I was having none of it. Then he had this great idea. He said he would drive me back home, and I did not have to walk. That was a great idea. He was finally getting around to being actually useful. I thought that more people needed to be useful like that. Needless to say, I ended up being tricked into going to a hospital the next day since my family could not figure out what else to do with me. When I remember back to that time, I imagined I was more than a handful. The thing about being bipolar is, you may not remember all that happens. I had to get most of this from my parents and my family, and I coupled that with bits and pieces of what I remembered. I still think they sugarcoated much of it. I don't blame them for it. You cannot imagine what is going through someone's head when they think they are the king, Jesus Christ, and God knows what else in just one night.

The hospital wasn't the end of it either. I thought that the guy in the bed next to me was the guy running for Attorney General of Michigan and that he was completely against medical marijuana. I had assumed that he would be looking for me, given how I grew and sold marijuana over Craigslist, and so began yet another dip into paranoia. I promptly told him to stop looking at me, and after I did, I thought that I had made things worse by calling attention to myself. I thought that I was being more suspicious than I should have been and that this newly anointed Attorney General was not onto me. My paranoia was at its peak. I was soon shifted to the psychiatric ward. A special place just for me, not having to share a room with anyone. I deserved it. You cannot expect a king to share his hospital ward with another stranger. I didn't, but strangely the people in the hospital found that observation amusing. Having my own room didn't last long as I was put in a room with three other guys shortly after arriving.

I was given medication three times a day. I started to spit it out, so they shifted to injections. I was given Risperdal and Seroquel. Risperdal is an anti-psychotic, and Seroquel is a mood stabilizer. After the doctors were able to determine that I was doing better, they released me. That was my tenth day in the ward.

After getting out of the hospital, I argued with my parents to get some more time with Laura, but she ended up blocking me instead and found someone from her past. She is married to him now.

Eventually, I was diagnosed as being bipolar, although I didn't exactly believe it to be true. I had weekly appointments with a psychologist and a psychiatrist to help me with my disorder. It was weird to be diagnosed at 32 with no previous indications of the disorder. It was determined that I was Type 1 bipolar, which means that I suffer more from mania than from depression, and the thing I underwent at the festival is called a manic episode with a psychotic break.

I didn't like that I was being given medication for it. I didn't see why I had to take such strong medicine for something that I determined was a one-time thing. However, I was proven wrong in the future as I did get manic episodes again, and the medicine has actually helped me fight my episodes. I'll get to that soon, but first: I need you to understand how I felt throughout the episode so that you can actually grasp what my mania felt like and how real it felt to me, even if it was anything but. As I may have said before, the truth mattered little. What I felt during these manic episodes was the truth for me. If I thought I was a king, I felt like it. The situation around me did not matter.

See, I am able to recount things perfectly here, but they're not my perspective. They're an outsider's perspective. As I said before, all of this is what I was told by my parents and Laura and Justin, and other people. In my mind, everything was entirely different.

In my mind, when I thought that I was being tracked down by the candidate for Michigan Attorney General and that it was all real. Actually, I did not think it was real. I knew it. I did not have to convince myself that what I felt, or what I thought, or what I knew, or what I thought

I knew, was anything but the truth. There was never a shadow of a doubt in my mind. What I believed was what I would see. I actually felt that I was being watched and tracked and followed. I actually felt that he was there, and he was trying to get to me. I actually thought that I was going to be in deep trouble with him and that I needed to escape. I actually felt that people were chasing me. The paranoia meant that every fear of mine was very real to me, and I felt the full force of it. I was actually scared and wanted to get rid of the people on my tail even though none of them were real, and my mind had created the scenario on its own. This goes in direct contradiction with my mania at that time, where I thought I was a king when I thought I was Jesus Christ himself. You might understand the overwhelming feelings that might be coming to me then, of the highest of highs and the lowest of lows. You are the king of the world in one moment and a helpless little pawn in the game of drugs and crime the next.

Similarly, when I thought I was seeing symbols or that I was Jesus Christ, it wasn't just me pretending to be any of that. I actually felt like that was who I was. In my mind, I actually was those people. In my mind, nothing was out of the ordinary. I was simply being normal, and there was nothing weird or odd to my behavior. I did not think about whether anything I did or thought was the truth. I did not think it wasn't.

Parts of it were a blur too. I don't even remember shouting at my dad, but I was told that I did so. The mania affects you in a lot of ways, and you tend to do things without any second thoughts to them. You don't get the time to think about your actions or what you're doing. You forget who you are and no longer have a sense of it. You are what your mania makes you, and more often than not, it is something on a grand scale, and you don't even realize it. You end up spending money or shouting at your family, or thinking that you're the king. It's unpredictable, and the psychosis can be scary once you realize that you could very well be doing the more irrelevant or inhumane things, and to the manic side of you, it would not matter. It gets scary when you think you can end up in jail, having done unspeakable things, and that a history of drug use and DUIs would not help my case.

I think it's difficult to explain to anyone how it feels true and real - not surreal, not like an out of body experience. You have to be in my head to understand the emotions as they truly were. But at this point, all I can say is that it's not like you're playing Jumanji, it's like you're sucked into the game itself, and all of it is very real to you. You aren't an observer or an actor, you're an actual part of the scenario that you have created, and you feel every bit of it. When the stampede hits, it kills you. When the hunter shoots, you die. You might lose years of your life, except this time, you realize that you will never return back from the game. You got sucked in, and you can never return. That feeling, when you take into account the rollercoaster of emotions I already felt, makes every waking moment a nightmare. You cannot know if you ever truly wake from it, and you cannot even go to sleep, as you might just go back in and never be able to come out of it again.

With that being said, that was not the last time that I had to face the manic episode. There were quite a few other bad ones too, that led me into situations I wanted to avoid. I cannot say if they were manic or hypomanic, the latter being a less severe version of the two, because they all felt severe to me. I had no control over my actions in those times and often did them for putting on a good show or getting some attention or out of beliefs that I held. If I did not get whatever unrealistic thing I wanted, I would become irritable.

It was near Mother's day in 2014 when it happened again. I started getting a little manic again. On that day, I was running around trying to make a pizza for my mom. I was sitting in the backyard in a lounge chair looking up at the clouds. My father came outside to check on me and I asked him if the clouds were moving since I thought that time had stopped. This time, I thought I was an alien from another planet. It got worse, and I found myself admitted to a hospital again.

My grandiose behavior caught up with the psychosis, and once again came the time when I was the most important person in the world, possibly the universe. No, definitely the universe. I thought Dr. Dre and Eminem would come to visit me in the hospital. They were just around every corner just waiting to jump out and surprise me. Well, that didn't exactly happen, but I did get help and start to feel better, and eventually found my way out of the hospital. This was also where I met Char.

I had my third episode a year later in 2015. This time, the mania hit a lot stronger, and I stayed awake for just about ten days. I thought that I was Jim Carey from the movie "The Truman Show" and was being watched at all times. Naturally, I wanted to put up a good show for the audience, and Jim Carey is nothing if not a good show. I over-exaggerated things. I made faces, did some method acting. I refused to be acknowledged by my own name. I actually thought I was Jim Carey and got confused when so many people around me used someone else's name to refer to me. I felt like it was a prank that they had all gathered and collectively decided to make me feel like I truly was from The Truman Show.

This time, the psychosis and delusions went way further than they ever did before. I thought that Taylor Swift and Katie Perry were fighting over me. I placed CDs on my windowsill at certain angles to reflect light to communicate with the sky people. During sundown, I would shout a bit louder, thinking that the fading sunlight meant that the sky people might not be able to hear me properly. At night, I would cry, thinking that they must feel like I think that I am better than them as I had gone radio silent. I was afraid they would retaliate. I even took down my mirror for some reason. It was a mess! Worse of all, I started to broadcast all of these thoughts on Facebook, which obviously didn't go well since none of this was actually real, even if I didn't know so. Some thought I was writing a fiction journal about someone who had gone crazy.

I thought that the TV and the radio were trying to talk to me, trying to coerce me into giving myself up to them. I ended up breaking my TV, and I could not handle what it said. I also took photos of my room for proof that all of this was real. I tried to beat the spirits out of the thousand-dollar Sarcophagus that my parents had purchased, thinking that I needed to do it. I jumped out of the window to show the sky people that I wasn't afraid. I'm lucky it didn't hurt me too badly.

True to form, I ended up in the hospital once again, and this time, my illusions of grandeur became a mish-mash of what I imagined would seem like absolute nonsense to an outsider. The jump didn't hurt me, but I was obviously manic and needed help. It took eight days for me to recover this time, and I was then discharged.

The fourth episode was in 2016. It clearly had become a yearly recurring thing for me at this point. This time around, it wasn't too bad. I did get all manic and wrote the first 40 pages of this book and also started to post things to Facebook again, but that was about it. I was discharged in five days. I believed that the novel I was writing was being edited for approval by Sir Arthur Conan Doyle and George Orwell. A strange combination, I know, but I felt like they had taken a liking to my talk of being on the run from them and the mystery of my book.

My 5th episode was in July 2017, and this time, the police were involved. I've discussed it in the previous chapters since it involved me driving under the influence. This is when I got beat up by seven cops in Austin. I wanted to post the police footage to Youtube, but Travis County has some kind of law against it.

The 6th episode lasted through March and April of 2018 and actually went on for quite some time. It was a particularly difficult one for my parents since they had to deal with a lot throughout this episode.

What happened was that we moved to Florida to escape the cold winter in January. So far, so good. However, things took a southward turn in March, when my mania started to get a hold of me again. This time, I went to ancestry.com and started to look up my relatives on it and complete my family tree. At this point, I was looking for my cousins twelve times removed and trying to track them down. I would disappear for a few days, and my parents were very concerned. They could not understand it now, but I thought they would in the end. I was on a quest to reunite our family.

The mania started to get worse, and I let our dog loose from the leash. Mom was able to find him after some trouble. Another time, I was loudly playing music to the neighbors, which I'm sure they didn't appreciate. I just thought it was in poor taste not to mix some rap music with a few loud guitar riffs like Metallica or the drums of Black Sabbath.

That was only the beginning, though, as things actually went a lot worse. I went to a park, taking the car along with me, and ended up thinking that I was talking to the birds. I then also thought it was appropriate for me to take down the U.S. flag because I thought it was going to be replaced with a new American flag. I obviously had quite a crowd of patriots gathered around me, shouting at me. The police soon arrived and put a stop to it. The cops called Justin for me, and my father and brother then had to come to pick me up. My car wouldn't start because the battery had been drained due to the breathalyzer, and my dad had to get a new battery and had my car towed off. It was obvious that I was manic again, and my father didn't want to wait long before he got me to the hospital this time. He knew I could be a lot of trouble to handle.

We went to the hospital the next day, where he left me to check myself in. I went and got my blood drawn instead. I have to get my blood drawn periodically to ensure that it doesn't clot. I then went out to look for my father but didn't find him there. I went to a smoothie shop instead and started smoking there inside the shop. The girl behind the counter asked me to go outside for a smoke if I wanted to, but I started shouting at her and refused to budge. The police were called, and one of them happened to be the ones that came to my place the previous day when my parents had called the cops over to try and force me to check myself into the hospital.

I was put in jail for resisting arrest. In trying to avoid being behind bars, I began building a jail of my own, with me inside of it. No matter what I did, I would sooner or later find myself locked in a cell. Of course, it could have been avoided, but my mania prevented me from that happening, or at least, that is what I told myself. I found the jail to be very uncomfortable. The paper cloth that I was given was not helping with the cold and tore off soon after they had given it to me. I felt I was being detained for no reason and that I was being treated unfairly. I was in isolation for a week with no clothes on. I was then taken to the hospital. After I got discharged, my parents decided to go back home since I was manic, and they didn't want to stay in Florida at the time with me acting out.

We were on our way home and stopped in Georgia at a motel. When we arrived, I asked my dad for the car keys saying that I wanted to grab something from the trunk. Instead, I drove the car off and slept in the car on some rural road. I tried to get back in the morning but couldn't find the way to the motel. At one point, I thought it had disappeared, and the sky people had taken it away in anger, now that I did not talk to them anymore.

I asked for directions to the Red Roof Inn but had driven off too far and was thus directed to a different Red Roof Inn. The one I was supposed to stay at was 30 miles off! I found a door ajar and thought it was my room and went in and got myself a bath. I then lay down in bed but was soon woken up by the phone ringing followed by knocks on the door. The police were there and wanted my ID. I had left it behind at the hospital.

I refused to open the door, but the officer kicked it open, and I was charged with trespassing and obstructing a police officer. I was taken to the Georgia jail, and a bond of $3000 was set on me, which my father paid and got me out on the 6th of April. What's even more interesting is that my parents had never stayed at a Red Roof Inn at all, and I had simply assumed that they had! I got year-long probation for this incident.

With that, I now drove back to Michigan with my father, and I thought that things would settle this time around. Well, guess not! I was still hooked on ancestry.com and traced some of my relatives in northern Michigan. I booked two separate hotel rooms for some reason and drove off into the night.

I was driving around Northern Michigan aimlessly, when I saw a herd of deer and started to flash my light at them. It was around 6 am and still dark out. I must have forgotten to turn my lights back on because I only had my fog lights on and I was soon stopped by the cops. They found a marijuana pipe in the middle counsel of my car and conducted field sobriety tests on me. I didn't have any weed on me, but that hardly matters when one is caught in the precarious situation I was put in, my only explanation being that I am either Jesus Christ himself, or got lost in trying to find a way to talk to the sky people. No matter what I was told, I was sure that I could find a way to talk to them, to finally be able to communicate. It was not as if the sky people were made up. These people just did not want me to get my way.

I was put in jail for a week. I waited for my parents to bail me out, but they didn't do so immediately. I suppose they were waiting for the manic episode to end before they did, and I don't blame them. I was let go for no bond eventually, but the judge decreed that I had to put an ankle tether on myself for now. I suppose it was fair.

If anything, it would give them the means to chronicle my adventures.

I didn't have much cash on me, so I had to use a Walmart phone to get my mom's credit card info. I was then able to book a room, get some food, and eventually get back home to Detroit to my parents.

What's interesting about all of this, and the many incidents that I have mentioned in this chapter, is that I never really had any control over my actions. Yet the episodes can be so bad that even a single episode in 2018 was enough to land me in jail three different times across three states! As it might be obvious, it isn't exactly easy to deal with your mania, and bipolar disorder really is no walk in the park. The worst part, I think, is the fear of the worse. At times, it is not even thinking, but knowing that the worse might just be yet to come, and you will have no idea when it does.

You might be completely okay one day and going about doing something, and then it would strike you with no warning. It will make you think about things that aren't really assumed to be as real as the ground beneath your feet and the fact that nobody had bowed down to me in quite some time. In these moments, the line between what is real and what isn't is blurred, eventually fading away into the only reality you know. You can go from silently working on your job and earning some good cash to suddenly going batshit crazy and not knowing what you are doing or why you're doing it. You can go from not believing in religion to believing that you're Jesus Christ overnight, and you won't even know the difference because you won't know what hit you. Logic and mania are not opposites, they simply do not exist in the same realm. You'd think that you're acting perfectly sane and normal and that there is nothing wrong with you, but everyone around you could clearly see that you're far from anything considered to be normal. That is how profound the impacts of the disorder are, and after you've worn out your disorder and have some time to reflect on what you've done, you realize how much of a hold your mania had on you and how little control you had over it yourself. The worst part of it doesn't come during the episode, but when you are truly yourself, the real you that has now realized that you are suffering from mania and psychosis. It isn't exactly easy to deal with, and I wouldn't want to wish it on anyone else because having lived with mania has proven to me that it can come and sneak up on me at any time, and I won't ever know what hit me or what happened to me.

See, it isn't exactly an easy life, but friends and family can always help and ensure that they can make it better. The love of your friends and family means a lot, and it can go a long way in helping you cope with the disorder and work on making yourself better. There are some things that you can do if your friends or family suffer from the disorder to make their lives easier. No matter if your disorder affects you the worst, simply having the empathy and sympathy to understand and relate to others can make it bearable for quite a few people.

The first thing that you can do is try to understand the disorder better. It's understandably difficult to put yourself into the shoes of someone that suffers from mania, but the more you read about it, the easier it gets to understand and the more helpful you can be to someone that has bipolar disorder. When someone acts a little less themselves, it might be best to play along, to indulge them in their fantasy, and try to help them that way. I am not saying bow down to me if I think I am king, but that if you do so, trying to help me, convincing me to check myself in a hospital, and letting me be more agreeable and tolerable, it helps things ever so much.

Educating yourself is so important because bipolar disorder can take so many forms and affect people in so many different ways that it can often be complicated and difficult to see through it unless you know exactly what to look for. You would not think that a stranger suddenly thinking themselves to be an alien from another planet has bipolar disorder; you would think they are crazy. The mania can go high or low, the person can get depressed, or there can be psychotic breaks to it. It's very difficult to grasp bipolar disorder despite how common it is truly,. That means that educating yourself becomes very important. The chances are that you know someone who is bipolar, but you simply don't know it yet because you haven't learned about it, and you simply tag them as crazy. However, it is also important not to self-diagnose. Remember to look out for them but not to assume things without reason. Misdiagnosis, even if it is not official once received by a doctor, can have unprecedented long-term effects.

Another thing that you can do to help someone that has bipolar disorder is to simply listen to them. It might seem like something very mundane, almost irrelevant in the grand scheme of things, but if you only listen to someone, they'll feel like they at least have some support. You don't need to have all the answers, and it's honestly almost impossible to have them in so many instances, but if you only lend a listening ear to them, it can be very helpful.

You can upscale your listening by adding in some support for the person that is suffering. When you're bipolar, you often feel like the world is against you, and you're being chased. In my example, I thought I was being watched at all times, which did not help with how I felt. I thought that the people were trying to chase me and get to me. Other people that have bipolar disorder can feel the same way too, and if you simply tell them that you're on their side and are there to support you, it can make them feel so much better since they know that you'll be there to help them and they aren't all alone in their suffering.

Another important thing that you need to do is to ensure that you help the person that has bipolar disorder by scheduling their appointments and convincing them to go to them. When you have bipolar disorder, you might often feel like you don't need the help or the treatment and that the episodes are a one-time thing. My experience proved that this was not the case and that the medicine helps a lot, as do the sessions with the therapist. Ensure that they go to their sessions, and ensure that they are getting the medical help that they need. Since this is a disorder, medical help is essential to treating it!

Perhaps the most important thing that you need to remember when you're dealing with someone that has bipolar disorder is not to lose your patience. I know that it can be tough to deal with someone that would make stupid decisions, possibly land you in trouble, or try to attract attention, but trust me, those actions are beyond their control, and they are not conscious decisions. You cannot punish them for what they did due to their disorder since it simply isn't in their control. If you blame them for it, they would feel guilt and feel bad. Your job should be to support them, and you should know that none of what happened was intentional.

Patience isn't always easy, but patience is the key to helping someone that has bipolar disorder. If you're patient with them and explain what they did wrong to them rather than bash at them, they'll be understanding and try to get the necessary help to ensure that they don't slip into manic episodes or psychotic breaks again. Getting them the help is critical, and blaming them gets you nowhere and is unfair to them since they did not consciously do any of what they did.

With that being said, don't forget that you're human too. There's only so much that you can do to help, and that's okay. Once you've given them the best that you can, you should step away. You shouldn't let your friend or family member drain you. You need to give your own mental health some priority as well. Help them, of course! You should never abandon them! But don't be afraid of stepping away from them too, if you need to for your own mental peace. The noises in your own mind are sometimes too loud to focus on anything else anyway, and the same can be said for others. People are always dealing with problems that others cannot understand, and even if yours are far worst, it does not give you, or anyone else, any sense of superiority. I am not trying to bring anyone down, or say that their problems don't matter, but that if someone's world is ending, sometimes they need to apply a few band aids to the problem before they are open to listening to you.

Chapter 12 – California Dreaming

Back in 2011, about a year after Laura left me and I had my first episode, Justin and I began pulling plants out of the grow house and trimming them back at my parent's house. All of the trim that I had been collecting filled up a 5 gallon bucket. We set up a day to go over to a guy named Brian's house in Detroit to make Butane Honey Oil (BHO) with the trim I had accumulated. Brian had set up a contraption that made the process faster and easier. The basics behind making the BHO were to fill a PVC tube up with trim and have a cap on each end. The caps have a tiny hold in each one on the tip and the bottom of the PVC tube. We had purchased a case of butane canisters for the project and used one can per batch of trim in the PVC tube. The butane can was used on the top cap and would force the THC trichomes out through the bottom hole. It made a concentrated oil called honey oil.

When Brian finished up, we had over 30 grams of BHO and we cut off a nice sized hunk for him to keep as payment for helping us out. It normally sells for about $40/gram, but we didn't plan on selling any of it. I had purchased a vape pen that held the oil in cartridges and we planned on bringing it with us on our trip out west. 30 grams was roughly a ball of wax a little bigger than a golf ball and worth between $1,000-$1,500. After I harvested the last of the plants, Justin and I made a few trips to the grow house to grab equipment.

By that point, I was so over the grow operation. We only took the most valuable equipment and left the rest for Pearl. She was my cool landlady for my grow house in Warren, Michigan. I had spent so many hours of my life in that basement and the payoff had pretty much been nonexistent. We took the lights and all of the tools that I had accumulated and left most of the buckets along with some of the other equipment I didn't want to fuss with behind.

After I finished drying out and jarring the weed, we packed up Justin's Lexus and hit the road. We took a few ounces of weed and the 30 grams of BHO with us. We brought some clothes and Justin brought his fan that he couldn't sleep without. We left Michigan heading for Arizona, but we were in no hurry to get there. Justin was considering moving to Arizona and wanted to check it out. Our friend Jamie and his wife Jennifer said we could stay with them for a while in Prescot, Arizona.

We weren't only going on this cross country trip to scope out Arizona. We also planned to get off of the Oxycodone pills we were hooked on. Justin had brought his last vial with him and the plan was to run out of them while we were on the road. Considering that we wouldn't be able to score anymore, we would be forced to quit and face the withdrawals. Neither of us looked forward to that, but we had decided to get off the opiates and this was the road we took.

Since we weren't in a hurry and had no were particular place to be, we drove for about 8 hours per day. This was much more comfortable than driving the 10 to 12 hours per day trying to get to a destination in record time which normally would have been our routine. We had the open road ahead of us, more than enough weed, and we were constantly using the vape pen to hit the BHO.

As we travelled across the country, we didn't stay in any city more than one night until we reached Moab, Utah. The beauty of the city had blown as away, so we decided to stay for a couple of days until we were ready to beeline it to Prescot, Arizona. We had been gone for about a week and were looking forward to sgetting off

the road and staying with Jamie for a few days. As we
made our way to Prescot, I noticed road signs directing us
to the Grand Canyon. I tried to convince Justin that we
should take the hour or so detour to check it out, but he
wasn't having any of it. I couldn't believe he wasn't
willing to go out of the way just by an hour in order to
see the Grand freakin' Canyon. That's just the way he is
though and being on drugs didn't help any. He was
basically unexcitable.

We stayed with Jamie and his wife Jennifer for about a
week in Prescot, Arizona. While we were there, they
showed us around the town and we spent a lot of time
smoking the BHO and the weed we brought. That was
kind of our offering for letting us crash with them for the
week. While we were there, I had contacted a second
cousin of mine that lived in Los Angeles. His name is
Dan and we are second cousins, which means that our
grandfathers were brothers. We weren't close at all and I
only remember seeing him a few times as kids, but I
figured I'd reach out to him anyways and see if we could
come for a visit. We hadn't even planned on going to
California, but when he responded to my Facebook
message enthusiastically, we thought it would be fun to
reconnect with him. Jamie and Jennifer had been arguing
a lot and Justin had had enough, so we left after a week
and made our way towards California.

Once we reached the Los Angeles area we began to
look for a motel that was reasonably priced, because we
had planned on staying for a while and Dan and his wife
Cindy live in a studio apartment and they couldn't put us
up. The first motel we found was near LAX airport and
was part of a chain, so it was about $100 per night. We
settled into our room and made plans to meet up with
Dan and Cindy the next day. We were beginning to run
low on Oxycodone and neither of us were ready to go
through withdraws, but the time had just about come.

The first week we were in LA, we did it up pretty
much every night. After spending almost a year of my

life living with my parents with no way to get around, I began to feel alive again. We went to the X Games in downtown LA, a few live music shows, and some cool restaurants and bars. We still had a bunch of the BHO and weed left, so you can just assume we were high all the time. Justin had asked Dan about scoring some cocaine and he said he would look into it for us. One of the following nights, Dan came over to our motel room and the three of us did a bunch of coke that Dan had gotten from one of his connections. Dan had also introduced Justin and me to DMT one night at his apartment after the bar. We had never heard of it before, but we were willing to try it after hearing Dan describe it is a psychedelic drug that only lasted a minute or 2 after smoking it.

Dimethyltrypteamine (DMT) is a chemical substance that occurs in many plants and animals and which is both a derivative and a structural analog of tryptamine. It can be consumed as a psychedelic drug and has historically been prepared by various cultures for ritual purposes as an entheogen. Rick Strassman labeled it "the spirit molecule". DMT is illegal in most countries.

We sprinkled some of the orange powder onto a bowl of weed and hit it just as you would normally smoke a bowl of weed, except you try to hold a hit as long as you possibly can. Once you exhaled, you would start to feel it immediately. It was similar to a super short and intense LSD trip. Dan did the first bowl as Justin, Cindy, and I looked on and he seemed to be in his own world after exhaling his hit and was seemingly unable to speak. Justin and I shared glances from across the room and couldn't help but to start laughing. Next up was Justin and after he exhaled his hit, he started laughing and he was able to talk. I was able to talk after taking my hit too. The walls looked as if they were melting to me. It felt like an intense LSD trip. It had a chemical taste to it and that was the only negative I found. It was most likely left over from the extraction process.

It was approaching July and we had finished off the last of the Oxycodone pills. We were still staying at the motel near the airport and we were getting on each other's last nerve. Justin kept calling our mother to complain about me and then I would have to speak with her and listen to her try to smooth things over between the two of us. Justin had some Suboxone pills, which are used to reduce withdraw symptoms for up to 24 hours, but he didn't have many of them. They are used to help opiate addicts become clean. We began to take some of those once we were out of the Oxycodone and they did help a lot. We had spent so much time with each other though, things were bound to reach a boiling point.

We were in our motel room and began to argue over something relatively minor, when Justin began to berate me over everything he could think of. This included just about every mistake I have ever made. I lost my temper and picked up his fairly heavy plastic fan that he had made sure to pack with him. He was in the doorway of our motel room and I threw the fan at him and a small piece broke off. We squared off to each other and I pummeled him. It was the first time I had ever punched him in the face and I had done it a few times. He told me to get my stuff and get out of the room, so that's what I did.

I walked down to the office to get a room of my own and he had followed me down there and began making a scene. The attendant was about to kick us both out, but I convinced him we would be OK. I moved my stuff into my new room and had come to the realization I'd be going through my withdraws without the aid of any more Suboxone. I waited about an hour and then called my mother to explain my side of the story and that I had to use her credit card for a separate room. The argument and subsequent fight was partially her fault for trying to get in between us and play peacemaker anyways.

The following day, we both woke up in our separate rooms and had cooled down a bit after each of us spoke with our mother. She made us realize we didn't have much choice but to get along. We were on a cross country road trip traveling in the same car. Justin had two black eyes from being on the receiving end of my punches. We had agreed that going through the withdraws had us both on edge and we weren't using our better judgment. When we went down to the office to notify the front desk clerk that we were going to continue our stay in the original room, the guy told us we weren't welcome to stay there any longer. Apparently, the commotion we had caused the prior night didn't sit well with the manager, so we had to pack up and look for somewhere else to stay.

Eventually, we found a motel to stay in that was around the same price as the one we had just left and it was a little closer to Dan and Cindy's place. It was in Culver City and the place was Brazilian themed. We were still going through withdraws and Justin was too embarrassed to hang out with Dan and Cindy due to his black eyes, so we kept to ourselves for about a week. I was getting frustrated because every day was like the one before it. We would go to bed planning to pack and leave the motel the next morning, but Justin would go down to the office around checkout time and tell them we were going to stay for another day.

I would wake up and be forced to hang around our dingy motel while Justin slept throughout the afternoon. I was disappointed we hadn't made it to the beach yet, because Justin was still going through withdrawals. We weren't even that far from Venice Beach, but it was impossible to get him to go anywhere. I was going through withdrawals too, but Justin's were worse, because he had been on opiates for much longer than I had. I'd grown pretty accustomed to going through withdrawals because I never had a constant supply like he had. I was always being cut off by him and therefor I was able to take it a little better than him.

Dan and Cindy picked me up a couple times during that week, so that I could get out of the motel while Justin was sleeping. One time we went to Venice Beach and walked up and down the boardwalk watching the street performers do their thing and another time they took me out to dinner. Not only was Justin hiding his black eyes, but we also wanted to keep under wraps the fact that we were withdrawing from opiates. Dan's our second cousin, but we barely knew each other at that point. As we came off of them, we began to grow excited about having so much to do in LA. It wasn't anything like the life we had been living for the past several years. All of a sudden there was so much to do.

The cost of renting a motel room was starting to wear on us, so we decided to come up with another plan. I looked on Craigslist to see if I could find a room to rent by the month and I came across many listings that had to be sorted through. Ultimately, after multiple phone calls and numerous emails, we whittled it down to two places. The first was a room in an apartment near Venice Beach. What made it attractive to us was the fact that we would be living with two European women in their 20's and the price was $700 for the month. The second place was listed as a luxury apartment with a fitness center and a pool that also boasted a view of the Hollywood sign.

Each of the listings were tailored to a single person, so it took some negotiating over the phone and through email to make it work with the both of us needing a place to stay. We were invited over to the luxury apartment building to meet the residents and to decide if it would be a right fit for all of us. We pushed their apartment buzzer and shortly thereafter we were greeted by Francisco. He had stepped off of the elevator with a glass of red wine in hand and wearing red denim pants and a loud floral shirt. He looked to be in his early 20's and of Mexican descent. The way he greeted us and spoke with us was very flamboyant. We took the elevator up one floor to the main floor and he showed us the fitness center, which happened to be right down the hall from their apartment. It was a fairly nice fitness center. It had a couple treadmills, a few other machines, and some free weights. Next, Francisco showed us the pool directly outside of the fitness center. It was a normal sized pool with a deep end of five feet and it was surrounded by pool chairs and a few tables.   I couldn't help but imagine what it would be like lounging at the pool with the other residents of the building.

Justin and I jumped on the place once they said it would be OK for us both to stay there.   Claudia was Francisco's roommate and she owned a restaurant called Sazon Latin Fusion in Culver City. When I met her, she had her back against the wall and was facing foreclosure. Every month in business was by sheer luck that Claudia was able to juggle the bills.   She made a hell of a empanada and her flan was off the hook. She fell victim to some bad reviews on Yelp and was unable to get them removed without paying Yelp money.

Francisco and Claudia each had their own room and Justin and I were sleeping in the main room on a couch and an air mattress. We were having so much fun in LA those first few weeks there, we were more than willing to sleep in somebody's living room as opposed to paying $100 a night for a motel. We lived in Korea Town, which is a part of LA. It's actually the part of LA that held the LA riots after the Rodney King verdict. Where I lived was real nice and was not too long of a walk to the bus stop. I'd hop the bus to hang out with my cousin Dan and his wife Cindy. Soon, I met Mondrian and he lived in West Hollywood, and I would take the bus to his house.

You may ask how come Justin didn't drive you over to Dan and Cindy's apartment. Justin lasted a week at Francisco and Claudia's apartment. He wasn't himself. He had gone through withdrawals and was now learning to live again and his brain was fuzzy. He kept parking in the wrong parking spots outside of our apartment building and he kept getting towed away. I think it happened three times and after that third time, he had just had enough and wanted to go back to Michigan to collect and gather himself.

I was having too much fun to go anywhere. I wasn't going back to my old bedroom at my parents house to sit on my ass for another year. I was going to make the most of my situation, so I told Justin I was going to stay. Even though I didn't have any money or credit cards to my name, I wouldn't budge. Justin had already paid for the whole month at the apartment. I might as well at least use that much if not more time there. After Justin left I had a conversation on the phone with my mother. She was understanding enough to understand how I felt about returning back to Michigan to live with her and my dad with no license to top it off. She was able to send me some money to support my lifestyle until I was able to figure out what the hell I was doing with my life and why the hell I was drinking in LA at 33.

Man, I had a great time in LA. It would have been much nicer to have a car to get around in, but I was able to make do without one. Plus, I didn't have to sit in the notorious traffic. They have an actual bus system in LA unlike in Detroit. Everything is messed up in Detroit. I went to a ton of concerts with Dan and Cindy and oftentimes Mondrian. Mondrian was from Sao Palo, Brazil and he sold all of his possessions and moved to Los Angeles. He had been a guitarist in a band back in Brazil and was anxious to find another band to be a part in. He studied English at the Kaplan school in LA and then went on to community college to study film.

The cool thing about him going to Kaplan is that his classmates were all young 20 somethings from other countries. Their parents had money and would send them to the Kaplan school in LA to learn English before returning home. We went to many parties and bars interacting with the foreign students. They liked to practice their English with natives, so I had a lot of strange conversations. The Japanese girls were the most fun. Every time they laughed, they would cover their mouths. It was funny to watch. We hung out with German and French women too. They may have thought of us as older creeps, but hey, my heart is still beating. I'm still alive.

I had run out of my medication that I had been put on and wasn't able to get anymore, so I stopped taking everything all together. I was taking other medication now and it included weed, LSD, ecstasy, DMT, and alcohol. My cousin Dan likes to drink, so I had a hard time keeping up with him. Dan was in a band called Maxi Wild and we would go watch them perform on the drums. We went and saw a lot of other shows too. Some that stand out are Shpongle, 311, and Fiona Apple. I was so psyched when I saw that Fiona Apple was singing live in LA, I went ahead and bought a ticket right away. It was the last of the money I had in my account, but I knew it would be worth it.

I've only been to two concerts by myself in my life. The first one was Eminem back in 2003. I had the night off from work at Fishbone's and I was able to score a ticket at the box office at the last minute. It was a handicap seat, but it made no difference to me. I made my way down to the floor near the stage. I couldn't use the bathroom or buy another beer, because I didn't want to lose my spot. Maybe I wouldn't be able to make it past security a second time. I had to pee so bad, I lifted up my shirt and peed into my empty beer cup with thousands of people around me. I'm crazy. The decision was rather easy for me.

The second concert that I went to alone was a Fiona Apple concert. I had been preparing for it all week. Let me tell you about an old iPhone I used to have. I no longer made calls with it, but I would use it with wifi for things like maps and email. I had a few pre-concert drinks and then made my way to the bus stop to bring me to the Greek Theatre. I waited and waited, but the damn bus never came. After waiting way too long, I was able to flag down a cab. This cut into my drinking funds for the night, so I was pretty pissed. Once I got to the concert, I had realized I missed about half of it. I was bummed, but I was still glad I got to see Fiona perform. I mention the old iPhone, because it would have been very helpful at the time. I was back to using a flip-phone though. Life was less complex.

I grew very close with my cousin Dan, his wife Cindy, Mondrian, and Claudia. It was a great time in my life and I only wish I had worked a little harder at finding gainful employment. I had a felony on my record since I had three DUIs and that negated my education and experience when it came time for the hiring process. I lived in LA for 8 months on my parents dime and I appreciate it so much. I would have lost my mind or done something else crazy had I been left to my own devices at my parents house. I badly needed an experience like living in LA to help me discover myself again. Mondrian called me Hunter S. Thompson one time when we were using DMT on top of a mountaintop. I had never been so flattered in my life. That's who I'd like to be compared to. I've definitely used drugs to open up my mind and help me understand the world around me.

My funds were cut off and I was forced to return to Detroit in February of 2013. I didn't blame my mother for forcing me to return home. It was time. The luster of LA had worn off, but I was really going to miss my cousin and Mondrian. I didn't have any friends to hang with back home. Everybody had moved onto doing their own thing. That's what happens when you grow up. You think differently as a kid though. You think your friends will be around forever, but eventually you grow apart.

Chapter 13 - Did I tell you About the Time I Went to Jail?

I woke up in the jail's medical cell, where I was kept under close inspection. It was good that they did because I was still in my own world. A surveillance camera loomed over my head, but it didn't really bother me. I was still thinking about the stripper that had given me three lap dances for $40 earlier that night, and I started masturbating to it, uncaring of the camera facing right towards me, watching my every move. It is one thing to run around in your underwear or believe that you have to talk to the sun people, and it is an entirely different kind of matter to turn towards public displays of self-affection. Finding these things about myself gave me a strange feeling. There is always a little bit of embarrassment that accompanies events like these once you get to know what you did. It was like being told about the events of a wild night after drinking heavily the night before. However, it was not just embarrassment that came to me in these moments, but shame.

A 25ish Mexican female guard ended up coming to my cell and asked me to stop, but I couldn't care less. I was already in jail, what else were they going to do? It was not that they could inflict any punishment, could they? That was until I remembered the restraining chair they had for people just like me and immediately complied with what the guard told me.

See, this wasn't the first or the last time that I would be going to jail. I had already gone to jail multiple times for DUI. This included the month-long jail time that I had gotten back in 2008 while I was still with Laura. I would go to jail in the future as well, including three times in three different states under a single, long, and drawn out manic episode. Such is life, right?

But each of those times, the jail was different in one way or another, and this time, it was a unique experience. I either had someone to come pull me out like Laura did, under a "work permit," or had short sentences that lasted only a few days. It made me think less of being arrested. I would just serve my time and get out. My experience with jail desensitized me a bit, even if it was for my euphoric self. I did not have to think about the consequences, and they were all too easy to deal with, I would think. I felt that a little bit of time behind bars is nothing to consider, and when I would go to jail, it would not phase me, knowing that I'd just get out soon. I know I'm saying the same thing over and over, but it helps drive the point home about how this experience affected me more than any other. This time, it was two whole months, and I was not prepared for what was coming for me.

I was suddenly facing the consequences of my actions, regardless of whether they were by choice or not. You see, it is not easy being bipolar. You blame yourself for things you had no control over, that you might never have done, and you are right to do so. Regardless of what happens, it is your fault, and you know it, and the only thing you can do is to amend those mistakes. But you can't because that other side of you never goes away, and those mistakes pile up and keep piling. You forget how you affect those around you, and soon, the lines between the real you and your other side begin to fade. It is slow at first. The process is gradual, like how a single manic episode once in my life quickly became a series of episodes ever-increasing in severity. You see, with each jail time came some sort of price. I paid the price in time, what little of it I did, but those that bailed me out, or got me away from the place on a work permit, they had to bear a monetary burden, and with jail sentences piling up, the process becomes more expensive in every way.

Before you can truly understand what happened, though, let's rewind a little bit. Remember the time when I got beat up by seven cops and was put into the hospital? The time when I had a manic episode and thought I could just lock my door to the cops, wave my middle finger at them, and make a scene? Well, it landed me in jail right after it landed me in the hospital. I cannot say that I make the best decisions in life when I am completely myself, that I am a great judge of character, or that if I am even confident and competent in what I do all the time, but nothing ever came close to the level of incompetence, of misjudgment, the point of having an over-inflated ego, than it came to there. If shame is what I felt after having to relive the events of the night before that landed me in jail, being told that I made that decision gave me a sense of pure disbelief. It was the kind that would make me wonder how anyone would be this idiotic, that they would think of themselves not only above the law, but would evoke that position as if they actually had it.

I was booked in jail in Downtown Austin. I had my mugshots and fingerprints were taken, which is always a treat. I felt like a celebrity at that time, thinking that it is paparazzi taking photos of me, and I can do little but display myself proudly. To an unknown spectator, though, it gave me the look of a man who had no regrets for what he did. Anyway, I was processed and ready to go into the cells. I then tried to find an empty chair to sit in the waiting area, but I didn't like any of the empty spots. There were criminals all over the waiting area crunched together. I went to grab another chair that was stacked up but the guards yelled at me and demanded that I put it right back down. I didn't want to comply so I was taken to a cell and locked up. I have no idea what I was doing in that cell, but they later came and tied me up to a restraining chair so that I couldn't move. This was not the throne I wanted. They also put a mask over my mouth so that I couldn't spit on any of the guards. Apparently, I had tried to do that already since they refused to give me the chair I deserved. I was basically trapped and had no way out. I didn't like that one bit.

Of course, I was frantic, on edge. Staying still, even when tied up and gagged, it was never going to be likely that I stay put. I had to do something. I was a little too uneasy. I didn't know what else to do, so I tried to tip my chair over, rocking it back and forth. It is like you rock your chair when you are bored, going back and forth, just a little bit more every time, edging closer and closer to falling down. You think that you have rocked just right, just enough that you come back down to rock it again, except you rock it a little too much and fall down. Well, it was like that, except that this time, I did not even think about falling. I kept rocking, little by little until I was finally able to go down. I did not think about what I would do after I went down; it was not as if I had a plan. I just wanted something to do. I passed out soon after and woke up in the medical wing. That's where the incident with the 25-year-old Mexican cop happened, and I wasn't exactly in a hurry to get back in that chair again. Soon after that, I dozed off again. It is a good thing that the rocking had given me a headache. It left me a little too tired to try anything else.

I woke up in jail to some rather low-quality bologna sandwich and an apple. The apple was fine, but the bologna, as much as I liked it, was just not something I would be willing eat if the situation were different. Any food in jail is just a little different. It wasn't great, but it was what they gave me, meaning whatever they offered was expected to be my favorite dish. I was not as lucky as some of the others, although my feeling of superiority over them was gone too. Other people had some money in their commissary and were able to buy themselves noodles and junk food and whatnot. Not me, though. I had none in mine, so I was left with what I could salvage from the jail food, which was far from ideal.

I was soon transferred with the rest of the inmates to a different section of the jail, which looked like a prison, but it wasn't as bad. The doors were open, and we could walk around if we wanted to, although I can say that it was not exactly a perk. There were TVs on each end of the pod that our cells were in, but they had no volume on them, or perhaps they had no speakers, to begin with. It didn't matter. All that mattered is that all we got was video, and we had to read the captions if we wanted to watch anything. If there were no subtitles, I could only hope that what was happening would be understood. It is not exactly captivating when you are lip-reading and guessing what is being said the whole time.

The commissary, I soon learned, offered more than just food items. It was more of a general-purpose provisionary shop, with the general-purpose items being anything they could get their hands on. Despite that, it was a neat little thing I found. Some inmates had grabbed themselves radios that they could use to listen to music or even the TV if they could tune the signal right. It wasn't exactly a quality stay, but in jail there is often more boredom and a general lack of anything happening that makes you hate the place.

Most of my inmates were Mexicans, with a few African Americans here and there. There were almost no whites. I did not expect that to change my time in jail as much as it did. The disproportionately high number of Mexicans meant that one of the TVs was permanently playing some Spanish channel, some novella that I couldn't understand if my life depended on it. I barely ever got the chance to grab the remote of the second one too, and I soon gave up trying. I simply had to watch what the others were watching.

There was very little else to do otherwise besides trying to watch TV. There wasn't exactly anything to do all day in the cells besides stare at the empty walls. Soon, I started to shower twice a day simply to wash some of the boredom out. But of course, that didn't exactly solve my dilemma. Soon, even that became ever so boring, and I still needed to find a way to keep myself entertained that didn't involve taking showers over and over again. It was not exactly like boredom outside of jail. You see, outside, you are not doing much of anything when you feel like this, but you have nothing else to do in jail. Your options are limited.

At least some things turned out in my favor. A good thing, too, since I wasn't feeling euphoric or grandiose anymore. A nice fellow inmate, a Mexican, noticed that I didn't have any money in the commissary and offered me some noodles. Even though I had to use some of the hot tap water, which was as good as you can expect, I enjoyed making them. They tasted delicious after the days upon days of nothing but bologna sandwiches and all the apples in the world. It was a huge upgrade and perhaps one of the best meals I have ever had. I wished I could get them more often, and the fact that I couldn't made that one meal all the more savory.

Another upside came when Latuda was added to my daily meal, along with the Lithium medicine that I was already prescribed and taking. This was supposed to help me with my bipolar disorder, so I was obviously not entirely pleased about that little happenstance. I don't really like medicine, hardly anyone does, and this started to reawaken that dreaded feeling within me. I guess the fear of reprisal kept me from having another episode, and I was able to contain that feeling.

However, my little jolt of fortune did not end there. I found out that every Latuda comes with a complimentary can of Nestle Boost. Well, that definitely boosted my morale! I could really have used some of that chocolate goodness, so I didn't dare complain. I quietly took my Latuda and then spent my time sipping through my Nestle Boost, savoring every moment of it. It made me forget all that laying around, the boredom of the day, the mind-numbing nothingness that happened all day, every day.

It had been five days now, and I had had no outside contact, which was starting to agitate me quite a bit. I didn't want to deal with the red ants that crawled onto my bed and the hunger pangs any longer. I realized then that it had only been four days, four! Two months of this was a little too much for me. It made me start to lose my mind. Luckily, I got my first visitor on my 5th day in jail. I think if not for that, I would have definitely had another episode.

I initially thought that someone had found out that I was in jail since my arrest was broadcasted, which made me feel euphoric. Those were my fifteen minutes of fame, which only encouraged my grandiose behavior at that time. Now, I had been taking my medicine, and I quickly let go of the thought. It felt much better having some kind of control over my actions now. I later found out that the policeman that had dropped me off at jail had gotten my brother's number from me when he had asked me for emergency contact and that he had dialed him up and let him know about my arrest and situation.

Finding out that I would get a visitor lifted my spirits. After days of not having anyone I knew to talk to, I would finally get some time with my family. My visitor was sadly not any member of my family, though. It was a lawyer that my mom had sent to get me out of jail. It was not as good as having a family member visit, but I was obviously still excited given how much I had wanted to get out of jail. The lawyer, though, had more troubling news to deliver for me as well. Apparently, my mom only wanted to get me released on the condition that I would go back to Detroit. I had spent a long time and a lot of effort in trying to come over to Austin rather than staying in Detroit, so I obviously wasn't pleased with the matter. The alternative option wasn't any easier either way, and I was left in between a rock and a hard place. My bail bond was set at $55,000 with a $5,500 deposit, and I would be in jail for at least three months while they analyzed my dashcam footage and tested my blood. As I said, I was stuck between a rock and a hard place. I saw no easy way out of it this time, no way to pay the bail and get out, no work permits, and no Laura to rescue me. The lawyer soon left and gave me time to ponder over what I wished to do.

Do you know how I talked about not caring about the consequences earlier? Well, this changed things. This time, things were not moving as fast. Life was not a blur anymore. The days did not go by, with every other day blurring into one another. This time, every second was an eternity, and I had all the time in the world to think about things. This time, my bail would be over sixty thousand dollars, and the burden was on my parents now. I started to wonder if I would ever get out. What if my parents cannot get the money? There was a $5,500 upfront deposit, and what happens then? Will I go back? Will I even be released before the bail is paid? All these questions made me realize how I was the cause of all this. Even if all of what happened was beyond my control, I could not help but feel guilty and accountable for it all. The harsh reality had caught up to me, and it was not letting go. Of course, when you are bipolar, the other kind of thoughts take over. I suddenly lost all my feeling of guilt and started to blame my mother.

I eventually thought that I should talk to my mother about it. I didn't understand why she would be doing this to me, how she would be so indirect and uncaring for me. I was beginning to get heavily frustrated at her and hateful towards her. 'The gall of this woman,' I thought. I was livid, no longer caring about how I seemed to her now. Angrily, I dialed her up collect from the calling room, and she picked up.

I asked her why she was forcing me back to Detroit when I had put in so much effort to escape and why she hadn't bailed me out yet. I did not think about how high the bail amount was. That part of the situation had all been forgotten by this point. The agitation in my voice was obvious. My mother told me that I had it all worked out wrong.

She told me that my health insurance was limited to Michigan, so it wouldn't cover for me while I was in Austin. She offered to let me go back to Austin once I had taken the treatment that I needed. She also said that she didn't exactly have $5,500 laying around with her, but she was working on it and that it wasn't easy for her. She told me that my father was scared of me, about how I would act, and about the damage I would do, so the whole arrangement would be very tricky to pull off. She told me that she was working on it. It was a conversation that calmed me down. It started as a fit of anger and turned into a moment of understanding. The annoyance gave way to sensibility after the call as some things slowly became clearer to me, and I hung the phone up. That moment of clarity made me hopeful, knowing that I would only have to stay in jail for at least a few more weeks while my family sorted an arrangement out.

In about two weeks, my mom had flown over, and she was able to get me out of jail the following Monday. She said that the judge had offered to let me go on a personal recognizance bond, so I would be able to go home as long as I promised to come back for the trial. Apparently, a personal recognizance bond means that bail is not required to get me out of jail. Going with that was a no brainer, and I just had to spend a few more days in jail.

The last few days in jail were sadly no less boring. If anything, they were awfully slow. I now knew that I would be able to get out of jail soon but still didn't get any entertainment. I think that I was now looking forward to getting out. The anticipation made the days go by all the more slowly. I was very excited about getting out but didn't exactly know what to do till then. A fellow prisoner told me how he tracks his weeks by how many peanut butter sandwiches he has left to go till he can get out of jail. They're served once a week, and they're my favorite jail snack. I'd take them over the bologna any day! However, I knew that I was going to get out in a few days, and I didn't need to count weeks at all, so I didn't see how that would help me. I thought that maybe I'd do the same thing with bologna sandwiches instead, but I did not want to go through with that either.

During my last few days in jail, my lawyer had come over and had some papers for me to sign for my release. He had actually come in on a Saturday, which was impressive. He told me that he would handle most of the trial and represent me himself, but I would have to come in for the final trial day. He also told me that I needed to have a breathalyzer installed in my car and was supposed to leave the state of Texas. I didn't think much about all of that anymore. I was just happy that I would be able to get out of jail in a few days' time, so a little breathalyzer in my car was not something that I particularly worried about.

Monday came, and my mom came to pick me up in her car. It had now been 14 days since I had come to jail, and I was now free to go. This was the longest I had lasted in jail. Normally I would be bailed out overnight or at least get a work release permit to ensure that I didn't have to spend most of my day in jail without anyone but the inmates and the guards for company. What were 14 days felt much longer than that, and despite only being two weeks, the world almost felt new to me when I got out. It was truly relieving to finally see the jail well behind me.

My mom had flown in on a plane and was going to take her car back home. My dad was going to take my car since he was scared of me and did not want to be with me. I had to go back home with my mom in her car. That stung. I didn't want my own father to be scared of me. I wasn't dangerous like that, just a little out of sorts at times.

I asked my mom for a cigarette and started smoking. I was soon talking and was very animated, which made my mom concerned. I soon picked up on it and assured her that I just hadn't talked to anyone in a while. I had to calm myself down a bit to show her that I was not manic, so she didn't need to worry. That seemed to calm her down a little bit, though I think she was still uneasy through the entire ride.

My mom inquired about what happened, though, so I told her how I had tried to get the police to pull me over and then got a beatdown by the cops. She was confused and asked me why I wanted to be arrested, and I told her that I needed the money that I would be getting by filing a lawsuit against the police for beating me up. She said that I made little sense, and I told her that logic was not my strong suit when I had my episodes. I don't know why I told her that. I don't think that's what I was really thinking. Perhaps the mania hadn't quite left me.

While I did end up going for the lawsuit, I honestly never intended on getting beaten up. I just wanted to do something interesting that I could write about in my book, and it had gone too far and led to all of this. I was still driven by the need to get the attention that I didn't need, and I was still doing things that were outright stupid to get it. Having stayed in jail for two weeks had helped me realize that. I think part of my erratic behavior was due to going to jail and being bailed out a little too easily a few too many times.

Staying in jail had actually helped me recognize a lot of things that I didn't think much about in the past. One of the most important of those lessons, I think, related to my family and how patient, loving, and understanding they had been. Whenever I found myself in jail I would always snap at them or be unhappy at them for not immediately getting me out, but I never stopped to consider how badly it must have impacted them and how difficult it must have been for them to do what they did for me. Having had a conversation with my mom and spending a few days in jail doing nothing but taking showers was an eye-opener though, and I could now clearly see how much love they had for me and how many times they had gone out of their way to ensure that I was doing well and not wasting my life. They had been more patient than I could have hoped for anyone to be.

Before all of this, I had been very blind to how much support they had extended to me. This was truly difficult for me to accept, but I knew it was the truth. I wouldn't have gotten anywhere if it weren't for my brothers and my parents. They were always patient with me and stayed with me, even when someone like Laura, who I thought was the love of my life, decided to leave me. They were there for me when I broke up with Teresa. They were there for me whenever I managed to land myself in jail, and they didn't think twice about paying my bond despite how much it must have cost them. They always took me to the hospital whenever I needed it, and my mom actively tried to get me legal help when I filed for bankruptcy or when I was detained. They never backed away from me, even though it was obviously not easy for them to come here and help me.

I had always thought that my family was very unhelpful and I deserved better. I thought they weren't always willing to get me out of jail and intentionally left me in there or didn't give me the support that I needed. But hearing the words from my mom's mouth made me understand the truth of the situation. The truth was that the outbreaks that I had were scary for them. The truth was that I had shouted at my parents and been angry at them and had broken their prized possessions such as their sarcophagus. But they never turned their backs on me.

The truth was that I was far from ideal due to my mental disorder. I had a lot of manic episodes that were very difficult for my family to deal with. It was bad to the extent that my own dad was now scared of me and refused to live with me. It wasn't because he stopped loving me. I know he still loved me dearly. It was because he was so afraid, he couldn't manage to be around me. I think that another reason was that he could not bear to see me like this, all sick in the head, though I think that his way of dealing with it was just different. I might have been the one with the disorder, but it had affected others around me all the same. It made me understand more and more about why he would be afraid. Perhaps it was fear, perhaps it was shame, or perhaps it was just the unbearable idea that his son wouldn't get better. It did not matter.

Or Maybe it was because he drove across the country from Detroit to Austin when he saw I was posting crazy things on Facebook, to see how he could help. I locked him out of the apartment at first and then let him in after a day or two. At one point, I had grabbed his fists and was playing 'why are you hitting yourself'. My dad is not a wuss. He'd kick someone's ass half his age and I'm sure of it. I had just crossed a line when I was playing around with him. I was able to get him to leave the apartment after that.

Before he was afraid, he had still done all he could and gone above and beyond to try and get me help. He had taken me to the hospital when I had needed it. Even when I got out of jail this time, he had been there to help me even if he didn't want to go home with me. He had gone to my apartment and collected my stuff and vacated it. He had driven my car home for me since I was going to go home with my mom. He had obviously played a pivotal role in ensuring that I got home safe and sound. Even at a distance, he would help me.

He was also willing to make financial contributions to get me out of jail. He was saving up for parts of the $5,500 that was meant to be paid, and then there would be the fee for the lawyer and the plane ticket as well. Those things don't exactly come cheap, but he didn't really care much about it. He just wanted his son to be safe and be able to achieve a better life.

My mom had obviously been my greatest support as well. She had tried her best to get me out of jail in every instance and was always there by my side. She had tried her best to help me even though she had suffered a lot in the process as well. She had never let go of me and had always stood by my side. I don't think I have appreciated all the people that have helped me enough. Even now, I have spent all this time talking about myself, about my disorder.

Another major support for me was my brothers, Scott and Justin. Scott had come to visit me in jail and had helped my mom and dad arrange for it. Justin had always been like a best friend to me and has been there for me whenever I have needed him. They've never judged me and have always wanted the best for me, and I'm really grateful to them for that.

See, the jail stay was very educational in the sense that it taught me that things aren't always the way they seem to be. I was under the illusion that my family didn't care enough for me, and I was all alone and on my own. And it's true, in a lot of ways, I was. They couldn't follow me into my manic headspace, and they couldn't do much to help with it, and I did have to suffer on my own. Of course, suffering on your own does mean those around you didn't suffer. They did, just in their own way. They might have never been able to understand what I went through, but the same can be said for me. I do not know what it is like to live with someone like me. I might have been alone in feeling what and how I did, but that didn't mean that they weren't trying their best for me.

I had thought that they were simply ignorant when in reality, I was the one being so. No one can magically get $5,500 overnight, and that kind of money was hard to come by. There are also legal restrictions, and my parents could obviously not have done much to help me. Of course, there's the added fact that they were traumatized due to how I had shouted at them and broken their stuff, among other things. They really wanted to help me, they just weren't capable of doing it at the moment, and that was okay.

I needed to have been open enough to see things from their perspective rather than keeping things limited to mine. My perspective was obviously impaired due to my mania, but that was the one that I had always stuck to, and I had never considered how difficult it must have been for them. But now I realized that things must be awfully difficult for them too, and now I knew that I had to ensure that I gave them my best too. I couldn't control myself during the mania, of course, but I could do so much better otherwise. I could take the necessary help, I could take my medicines, and I could be nicer to my parents. I could help them understand my condition, and I could listen to them when they ask me to go to the hospital and make things easier for them. And I could be grateful to them rather than thinking that they owe me something more. I could try to see things from their perspective and understand that they had actually put in a lot of effort for my sake, which isn't exactly easy.

I think the takeaway from all of this is embedded deep within me now. I know that I should be more open-minded and not be angry at the world. I know that being bipolar sucks, but that doesn't mean that it's the fault of those who are near or dear to me. If anything, they're the ones that make it better for me, and I should appreciate them. The incident showed me the truth in a way, and I am still very greatly affected by it. I have learned to try and calm down and try to understand things before letting anger take over, and it has helped me see that a lot of the times when I have been mad at others for not doing something for me, they had been trying their best despite not owing any of it to me, given how I was now 38 and supposed to be independent.

If I had not gone through this experience, I probably would have continued behaving the way I used to. I would have assumed that people simply didn't want to help me and would have continued being angry at them. Getting the perspective of my parents was hurtful for me, and it stung me to know that my own father could be scared of me, but it also helped me see that my belief was never true, and it helped me overcome my anger. It helped me see that my parents were trying their best for me, even if their best was a lot lower than my expectations, and I couldn't ask them to do anything more. It also showed to me that a lot of my friends and family have been trying to help me however they can, in their own capacities, and that I'm not alone. I now know that people have been trying to help me, and I simply need to have an open mind about it. Humans can't cure things overnight, but it's the effort that matters. And I'm truly grateful for all the effort that my parents and siblings have put in to help me, and I am lucky that I have always had their love and support.

We don't always see the truth for what it really is because we are often angry at the world or in pain. We think that the world is unfair to us, and honestly, it is in many ways. But that doesn't mean that everyone is out there to get you or not interested in helping you. Some people might be trying their best to be there for you, but you might not be noticing those efforts because you simply want more. You want someone to wave a wand and wish your troubles away. But that doesn't happen. We need to recognize the little things that people do for us and how they try to help us and be grateful to them for it. It goes a long way and can actually make you happier. Knowing that my family had my back, even if they couldn't always get me out of jail overnight, definitely made me a lot happier! The next chapter will focus on how the help I could get couldn't be absolute, and how I overcame that too, so read on! Sometimes, you have to be your own cheerleader, for people are very limited in what they can help with, after all. Had I never gone to jail, I would never have realized it, and I would have kept trying to rely on my parents and trying to get their help and then being mad at them for being unable to do so. I'm glad I

learned my lesson and started to work on myself and put
effort into my own mental health as well.

Chapter 14 – More Drugs

"*I used to use drugs. I still do, but I used to too.*"
-
Mitch Hedberg

My drug use isn't exactly easy for me to put on paper for the world to see, but I think it's an important element of my story. Some experts say that smoking marijuana can lead to bipolar disorder and others say that's not true. In many instances the person with bipolar disorder is self medicating. They know something is wrong with themselves, but they have never been diagnosed, so they use drugs like marijuana to make themselves feel better. I was diagnosed with bipolar disorder at age 32, but that doesn't mean I didn't always have it. I was only diagnosed after my first manic episode and subsequent psychosis. That was after the camping trip with Laura and Justin.

Ryan and Dan Minor were major influences on me at age 15. I was an influence on them too and not always a good one. They were both a year older than me and they were the first guys I ever got drunk with. We would take liquor from Dan's parent's liquor cabinet and experiment in his basement on Harvard. This was when I had my paper route and I started to wake up late on the weekends because I was hung over from drinking all night with Dan and Ryan. We would do shots of vodka, rum, gin, Tequila, Bailey's, and basically anything we could get our hands on. Dan's father, Dennis, was part of a wine club that made wine and it was super strong and fruity. We would occasionally crack a bottle of that when we were desperate.

When we had taken all the liquor we could from Dan's parent's liquor cabinet and watered down some of the bottles, we had to come up with other ways to get liquor. There were a few liquor stores in the neighborhood that we would go to and wait out in front. One was on East Warren called Liquor Island. We would look for a college aged kid or a person down on their luck, say, a bum, to purchase our liquor for us. It usually didn't take us long to find somebody to do it for a tip. Win-Win situation. We would drink the normal things teenagers drink like Cisco and Mad Dog 20/20, but for some reason we were into buying malt liquor. Crazy Horse is one that comes to mind and that stuff made you do crazy stuff! I didn't like the taste of beer or malt liquor, but I guess we figured malt liquor works quicker if you chug it down. Some times we would buy half pints or pints of cheap vodka and we'd all have our own bottle.

Ryan found some marijuana in Thom's house and him and Dan decided to smoke it. I was not down with it at the time, so I would get a couple 40 ounce beers and chug those while the two of them would smoke. Eventually, those two peer pressured me into smoking some marijuana, but I didn't feel anything at all. It took me a few times of smoking before I felt anything. Once, I did though, I was pretty much hooked on the plant. I left 8th grade the captain of the baseball, basketball, and soccer teams and started 9th grade as a burnout.

We got our weed from shady Ronnie who lived down the street from me on Cadieux. There was another guy named Bobby that would screw us over with parsley or simply run off with our money. We only fell for that a couple times because we were desperate. Once we started driving though we heard of spots in Detroit that you could drive and they would serve you in your car. We would go to the most dangerous neighborhoods in the world to score weed every single day in high school. We only got robbed once!

Missy, Justin, Rico, and me were going about our everyday habit of driving to Jane street near French Road to pick up some dime bags. When we pulled up, the kids decided to rob us. They pointed a gun at Missy's head and told me if I even think about driving away, they are going to blow her head off. I thought for a quick second about driving off, but I complied with their orders. They told us to get out of the car and they went through our pockets. Once they got all of our valuables and couldn't find the title to the car, they let us go and told us not to come back. They told us they didn't want us in their neighborhood because we brought the heat with us. We stayed away for a few days and then we were right back at it.

I used alcohol and marijuana throughout high school and basically throughout my life. The LSD I used I told you about already. There were many more doses taken after that time I wigged out in front of my parents as a teenager. I'd say over 100 hits, but I lost count and I have no idea how many more doses over that 100. I used pills only one time in my teens and that was around age 15. You may have guessed it, Ryan had found some of Thom's pills and was handing them out like Tic-Taks. I think it was Valium and muscle relaxers, but I'm not even sure what it was. I took these pills and did some crazy shit. We were on the garage roof of Chris' and I decided to dive head first into a pine tree that was next to the garage. I didn't think I felt anything from the pills, but that act proved that I did.

Pills weren't really around much when I was in high school. I would have known if they were and I don't think I would have been interested in them at the time even if they were available. I didn't touch another pill until I was age 25. I used a lot of LSD in high school and magic mushrooms too. I just loved the idea of expanding my mind. A dose always changes your perspective on life and can really be life changing.

Ecstasy was introduced to me by Teresa in 1999. We used it a few times together and I loved that shit. I wish I could feel like I was on ecstasy all the time. But you can't and that's the problem. It robs you of your tomorrow, because you feel depression for a few days afterwards. If you take too much of it over long periods of time, it can seriously mess with your emotions. For New Years Eve 1999, Justin, his girlfriend Ann, Teresa, our friend Brian, and I went to New Orleans to celebrate. Teresa and I were on ecstasy and having the time of our lives. I think about that night all the time. Y2K was going down and people were scared of what would happen when the computers turned over. Not us though. We hopped in Brian's car and drove down to Louisiana to celebrate the new millennium. We were always trying to capture these moments and this is one that I still have fond memories of over 20 years later. I still have the shirt I wore in my closet!

When I was living in Ypsilanti and going to Eastern Michigan University, I got pulled over on the way back from Teresa's house in Detroit when we first started dating. I had just picked up two ounces of marijuana and I was driving home around midnight. Two ounces is about the size of two softballs, so when I got pulled over, I didn't know what to do with the weed. I stuffed it down my pants and eventually had to come clean with the cop when he was patting me down. Arrested at 19 with two ounces of marijuana in Allen Park, Michigan. I got a year's worth of probation and had to do community service at some park in Allen Park. Add that to my rap sheet.

So, I've covered my marijuana, LSD, mushrooms, and ecstasy use. So far, so good. At age 25, I was working in a fine dining restaurant in downtown Detroit in the Renaissance Center, called Seldom Blues. I had to wear a tuxedo to work and it felt like prom every day. I was a waiter there and I was on my feet a lot. I started feeling a pain in my right calf and thought I had pulled a muscle. I felt this pain for a few shifts and then finally one night, Chris Webber, the former NBA star comes into Seldom Blues and sits in my section. I'm waiting on him and a table full of people and I'm limping around because my leg hurts. Chris told me I should have it checked out, so I did the next day and I ended up having a blood clot in my leg. I was hospitalized for a few days and had to give myself blood thinner shots in the stomach twice a day for a month. I guess I could have died.

The doctor had put me on blood thinners and told me I couldn't drink alcohol with them or else it would ruin my liver. Enter the pain pill, Vicodin. My friends were still hanging out in bars and I was too. I was 25 years old and still enjoyed the night life. Smoking weed and going to bars wasn't going to cut it for me for too long. I wasn't an alcoholic, but I would say I got fairly close to being one. I was never an everyday drinker or a morning or day drinker. For the most part, I only drank on the weekends, but I binge drank.

Justin, my brother, was in a car accident when he was 19. He was driving with Rico in my brother Scott's car on E. Outer Drive and hopped a curb. I think they were sharing a joint at the time, but I guess it doesn't matter. Justin drove the car head on into a tree in the median and fucked both him and Rico up. Justin is prone to car accidents because he's been in more than the average person over his life. His back has been messed up for a long time and he's always seen a pain specialist. Do you see where this is going? Justin has been getting prescribed Vicodin, Oxycodone, Fentanyl, and numerous other medications to deal with his pain for the last 20 years.

When I found out I could no longer drink, I wanted a way to maintain my social life so I went to Justin for Vicodin. I used to use it and nod off whether I was at home or out at the bar. I looked like an idiot and didn't even realize it. But I felt so good. It's a great feeling, but this is one drug I wouldn't recommend unless you need it for pain. It's easy to get hooked on, because it makes you feel so good. You want to feel like that all the time, but soon it's taking more and more to reach the level of high you want. The withdrawals are horrible, too. I've done it 100 times and it never gets better. You know what to expect, but it still sucks anyway.

At times, Justin would get mad at me for some reason or another and would cut me off from the supply of pills. This drove me crazy, because I felt he was responsible for getting me hooked in the first place. I would try anything I could to get my hands on those pills. Justin would buy safes and store his medications in there, but I would wait for him to leave and find a way to crack the safe. I swear, sometimes I amaze myself! I would crack his safe or get into the trunk of his car and grab a handful of pills. The times he found out, he was livid. Then we wouldn't talk for weeks.

The Vicodin turned into Oxycodone, which turned into Fentanyl. I kept needing something stronger to reach what first took me so little. Fentanyl is the drug that people are putting in heroin right now and dropping dead. I would take a patch that was meant to last on your arm for 3 days and tear it open and eat the liquid out of the patch. I was out of control. I could have dropped dead at any moment. Maybe I was trying to drop dead. My brother even had Fentanyl suckers he would eat out at the bar. He looked ridiculous.

When I could't get any pills from Justin, because he was mad at me for some reason or another, I found a way to order them online. It was crazy, but for a little while you were able to talk to a doctor over the phone in another state and get a script for Vicodin. You had to pay the postman COD, Cash on Delivery. It was expensive, but I was able to get what I needed when all else failed. I was hooked on these stupid little blue pills. They say Vicodin and Oxycodone are expensive on the street, but I wouldn't know. I never had to pay for them on the street in my life. I had my pharmacist brother supplying me for free. The only person I stole from was him!

Let me back up for a bit. I did attempt to steal from my high school friend Brad Marx. I was a desperate junky and he needed to use a fax machine at my house to withdraw some funds from one of his bank accounts. He left the fax sheet at my house, so one time out of junky desperation, I tried to transfer funds from his account to my account. I really feel awful about this. He was sure to notify all of our friends of my behavior and I was ousted and scorned from the group. Brad's no longer with us, but he forgave me before he passed. I need to forgive myself. It's not like the bipolar episodes where I wasn't in control of myself. This was different. I consciously made a decision to steal from my friend, junky or not, I had crossed the line. When he found out, he left me a voicemail message telling me the bank wanted to know if he wanted to press charges. He told them no, but he gave me a scathing message, which I deserved.

Cocaine is one drug I'm glad I never got addicted to. I've used it a little, but it's not something I ever craved. Teresa had a cocaine habit that she was able to keep secret from me for years. It sucked finding that out, but I guess it was her life to live. In fact the only coke story I have is about when we went to the Dominican Republic with my parents. Justin and I scored some from the bell hop and it was the best I had ever done. It must have been super pure compared to what I had tried in the U.S.

Last, but not leas, is DMT. I had never even heard of DMT until I lived in LA in 2012. My cousin Dan introduced it to me and I loved it. I was buying a couple vials a week and smoking it like I owned it. You sprinkle some on top of your weed and smoke it in a bowl. It's a hallucinogenic, so you know I was down for it. It comes from some tree bark, but it packs a powerful punch. My cousin was producing it and I was his prime customer. I'll tell you more about DMT and L.A. in an upcoming chapter.

My bouts with addiction are embarrassing, but at the same time, they made me stronger. I have been court ordered to go to Alcoholics Anonymous in the past for a real long time. I had to collect signatures for my probation officers. I realized one thing from going to A.A. and that is that I am not an alcoholic. Yeah, I may have 5 DUIs (3 drinking, 2 marijuana), but I'm not an alcoholic and I know this for a fact. I can drink one beer. I can drink no beer. I just got caught doing what I've always done and that's ignoring authority. I can't say it's a good way to live, but it is sure to add some excitement to your life.

Marijuana is the drug for me, but I am not allowed to use it because I am still on probation for getting arrested in Austin. I am not allowed to use any drugs or alcohol at this time in my life. If I screw up while on probation in Texas, I will do five years in prison. I would enjoy nothing more than to post the videos from the dashboard camera from the events of that night. I think the public ought to know about what happened that night the cops beat the shit out of me. Unfortunately, in Travis County, Texas, a person is only allowed to watch the videos in their lawyers office. They have a law so they can bury these types of police brutality tapes and avoid public scrutiny.

It's fair to say that if you pick a random day over the last 25 years, I'd be high on marijuana, as long as I wasn't on probation. In high school, I was voted most likely to fall asleep under a tree and wake up in 20 years. Well, here I am. Woke. I was sleeping in school because I was staying out all night hanging out with Eminem and his roommates.

Dan and I took some LSD the night we went to watch Eminem and Chaos Kid at Lakeview High School. They were opening up for a guy named Joe Joseph. Joe actually helped fund Marsh's first single and never received a cent.

It wasn't a talent show, but it was the likes. Joe had gone to Lakeview High School and was pursuing a music career, so he booked a show at his old high school. I was on acid, but I don't think Eminem and Chaos Kid were very good that night. The sound system was awful and you couldn't really understand them that well either. So, that's it for my drug history. I'm sure this chapter will help me secure work in the future.

Chapter 15 – You are Your Own Cheerleader

There are so many more stories I have to tell you, but only a little bit more book left. My editor tells me that most people want to read a book about 200 pages long, so here you go. Sometimes, Ryan or Dan will tell me a story about growing up together and I won't remember any of it. I mean the most outrageous stories you could imagine and I have no recollection. I'm going to have them help me out on the next book, because I know there is a lot of stuff that's missing. Not a bad recollection for the past 41 years, eh? I tried to cover as much as I could and make the story enjoyable for you.

One of the problems with creating a book over a 5 year span is that you tend to forget which stories you have told already and which ones you still have to tell and line them up accordingly. I didn't think telling my story chronologically would have been as interesting as jumping around and I didn't want my book to get boring. I've written a piece of this book everywhere from jail to the local Starbuck's. Most of it was written on my couch in my bedroom though using my MacBook Air.

Before I sign off, I want to tell you a couple more stories. The first one is about jail again and the second one is about Eminem's number one Stan fan, Alexis Mercier from France. He came to visit Detroit and coordinated a day to meet up with me for a drive and lunch. He had noticed that I was writing a book about hanging out with Eminem and his roommates and wanted to get in contact with me so I could show him the Wayburn house.

He's Eminem's biggest fan. He wanted to interview me on knowing Eminem before he was famous, so I agreed to do it. I have never been interviewed or really ever felt comfortable in front of web cams. I didn't know how much to give away in the interview either, so I kept mum about a lot of stuff. I guess it really doesn't matter. Alexis has made Youtube videos called 'Legacy' where he traces Marshall's tracks and takes photos of everything related to Eminem. He visits places that appear in videos and old houses of Eminem.

Adeline, his girlfriend, came with him to Detroit from France, so that he could gather more content for his videos. I took them down to Mexican town to get some food from Xochimilco and it was good. Looking back, I should have brought them to Buddy's Pizza, but they'll be back, so I'll do it then. After eating in Mexican town we went for a drive through Rochester Hills. Alexis wanted to show me Eminem's old house, so I obliged.

We pulled up at Eminem's old mansion and started taking some photos at the gate. After we had finished we hopped back into the car and had to turn around because the street was a dead end. As we were passing the house again on our way out, there was a guy standing at the gate with a freaking machine gun. He must be the new owner and not very tolerant of trespassers. We sped away from there and didn't look back. I promised Alexis I would put this in the book for him.

The longest stint I did in jail was 5 months in a Northern Michigan city called Petoskey for driving while having marijuana in my system. I already told you about spending the week in jail, but that was even before I was sentenced. I got sentenced to 6 months in jail and ended up doing 5 months with good behavior. That means they let you off early if you don't get in any trouble while you're in there.

For the first month I was in a regular jail cell with 2, sometimes 3 other people. This is while I awaited sentencing and counted towards my time served. It was me, Cody, and Dewey for that first month and we got tired of Cody pretty quickly. These guys were 18 and 20 years old. Cody wanted to keep playing rummy or spades and it was getting on my nerves. I can only play so many hands of a stupid card game. We had a TV in our cell, which was pleasant. There was a toilet in the cell that you never really get used to using in front of other people. The only time we left the cell is when they would sometimes come get us to go to the recreation room, which had a large screen TV and a bunch of tables. More cards!

After I was sentenced they moved me to the pods which housed about 10 other guys. It was like an apartment in a way or a cage, depending on how you look at it. At least you had privacy while using the toilet in this place. Somebody managed to get their hands on a Sports Illustrated Swimsuit Edition, which made for great fapping material in the shower. There was Kate Bock, Elizabeth Turner, and Samantha Hoopes adorning our shower walls. A guy can dream, right?

The pod had 8 beds on the top level and 8 beds on the bottom level, so it actually housed 16 inmates, but there were never that many in there at once. Every day was not that blur that you would hope for. Every hour lasted an eternity. We had a TV to share between the 10 of us, but they kept watching shows like Ridiculousness. That girl's laugh drives me nuts. My parents sent me money for commissary every month, so I was never in need of anything. It was quite the opposite. I would buy a bunch of crappy instant coffee so I'd always have extra on hand. That way I could trade a shot of Keefer coffee for other things, like food off somebody's plate. I had a deal with my cellmate Kyle. I would give him my hard boiled egg at breakfast time and he would give me his cereal. That's kind of the way it went.

All the guys in the pod know about the book. I would tell them some of these stories I've told you or something would happen in jail and somebody would say, "you should put that in your book". Kyle was my buddy in jail and Dewey was like a little brother. Dewey as he liked was only 18 years old and Kyle was 30. Dewey landed in there when he sold a bag of marijuana to an undercover cop in the sticks up north and Kyle was in for selling heroine laced with Fentanyl.

I stay in touch with the guys via Facebook now that we're all out on the street. It's hard doing time, so finding a few cool people always helps make the day better. The thing about jail is that you are forced to be around people you probably don't like. That was the case many times with me in jail. I just couldn't wait for them to get released. Once they were released, time went by a little easier. Instead of looking forward to my release date, I was looking forward to theirs.

After I served my 5 months in jail in Northern Michigan, I had to face the music in Austin for having marijuana in my system. I spent 2 more months in jail in Austin while awaiting my court date. That was pretty crazy. A lot of Mexicans again, but this time some of them had tattoos on their faces. It's hard to take somebody seriously that has a tattoo on their face, but I tried to. Those were a tough 2 months.

The cool thing about doing jail in Travis County jail in Austin, Texas was that they allow inmates to use tablets to listen to music, read e-books, listen to podcasts, and play games. I thought that was pretty neat, because I really enjoy listening to music. I read a little bit too, but nothing caught my interest and it was difficult to focus in there. Another four man cell was my home for those two months. My old college buddy Josh came to visit me in jail and I was really surprised. He's lived in Austin for quite a while now. He's writing a book right now too, you should look for it. He's a better writer than I am.

The judge placed me on probation for five years. I have a breathalyzer in my car that I can't drive parked in my driveway. I have to blow into it once in the morning and once in the evening. I'm also randomly drug tested weekly. I can try to get my drivers license back after two and a half years, but it's not certain. Bipolar disorder sucks. It feels like I'm paying for somebody else's mistake, but I do own it.

Our minds are a wonderful thing. They do so much. I know I am stating the obvious, but really, they are quite fascinating. My mind is different than yours. In fact, my mind is hopefully very different to yours. I don't think I need to reiterate why, but I will anyway. I have bipolar disorder, and if you did not know, a bipolar disorder is a mental illness. Mental illnesses are now more commonly described as mental disorders, and there is a reason for that. They mess with your brain, having you lose control of yourself in considerably inopportune times.

That is how my own mind got me in jail. It got me in trouble far more times than that, and it changed my life – often for the worse – even more so. But that changed. It took time, quite a lot of my life, in fact, but I got better. It did not happen magically or miraculously or through any particular treatment that I delivered, but through myself, through my mind. I got better as a result of how I began to think, and I began to think much differently.

Before I got better, I used to think things were hopeless. Bipolar disorder is not the most well-understood disease, and it is chronic, meaning that it will probably last me my life. It even showed up quite suddenly, so it was like a train had hit me. My world had turned upside down all of a sudden, and now it was experiencing seizures without warning. I would start to think in ways that would have been completely irrational to someone who had their thoughts together. My mental episodes were truly something else. If you want something a bit more descriptive, I think I wrote it best –

you know, from the context – in how I felt when I had my bipolar disorders:

"I felt high as a kite. At the moment, I felt like I could do anything in the world, I felt like whatever I did I would excel at it, everything felt good, and everything made sense, I was calm yet fast-moving."

You know what a wavelength looks like when it is visualized right? It is a series of ups and downs, and they are quite sudden. That is what I felt like. When I had these episodes, I was both the unstoppable force and the immovable object.

My victory over my affliction was not easy, quite the opposite. In fact, to say that it was difficult would be an understatement in of itself. Last time out I talked about the truth, about how we see it different from what it actually is. Our version of the truth is not the truth itself, but a variation of it. One can only imagine what kind of a shock it must be for someone to receive the news that they have been diagnosed with bipolar disorder. Unfortunately, I do not have to imagine it. Not only that, but I was in my early thirty's when it happened. It made me wonder. What kind of illness shows itself at thirty two? What ensued after that was me taking my medication, and they were strong. I mean, they were very strong. They made me feel like a zombie. I did not want to feel like a zombie my whole life.

By September of the year I first had my disorder, my parents had agreed to let me go back to my place in Royal Oak. Laura was gone now, and it was just me with almost no furniture and no car to get around with, but at least I was out of my parent's house. Emancipation from one side, and a kind of prison-like confinement in the next. I might have moved, but my life did not exactly change all that much. My mother would drive the 45 minutes to my house to pick me up and bring me to my grow house. She would read a book in her car while I did my work. She would also come over to take me grocery shopping when

I needed food. It couldn't last forever though. Having no means of transportation really sucks and makes life really difficult.   I moved back with my parents on November 1st, the following month.

Life was a struggle for me for a long time. I was disappointed Laura had left me, though I didn't blame her. She could have waited a little longer and maybe let me down a bit easier, but at the same time, I had lost my mind. When you have delusions of grandeur and are forced to come back to reality, it can cause quite a bit of a stir in your head. It's a long way to fall from thinking you're Jesus Christ – not some personification or a doppelganger type Jesus, but the prophet himself. To come to the realization you're a nobody and that your girlfriend doesn't want to be with you anymore, it can be eye opening, and not it a good way. I was having a very long bout of depression and the only thing that made me feel better was Oxycodone. You might have guessed where this is going.

My disorder had led to my life being in shambles, and that in turn, led me to depression, and ultimately, drug abuse. For the next 8 months, I didn't really do much outside of going to my grow house and to my doctor's appointments. I lived with my parents and counted on them for pretty much everything. My mother continued to drive me the 35 minutes to my grow house and then she would either wait or drop me off and come back and pick me up. The grow house was the absolute only thing I had going for me and my mother knew that. Without it, she wasn't sure what I would do, so I kept it going. Watching the plants grow was pretty therapeutic.

Justin was home from college permanently now, so we were popping Oxycodone and smoking weed all day, every day. We grew tired of going to bars and drinking so we would do other things like go to the movies and something even more lame; we would go to Dave & Buster's to play video games. Life was pretty boring. Justin began talking about taking a trip out west to

Arizona in the summertime, to check it out and see if he wanted to move there. His old friend Jamie and his wife, Jennifer lived in Prescot, Arizona so we figured we'd visit them for a while.

All these things were happening, and my condition was not improving. In fact, the sheer randomness of my bipolar disorder meant that I could not have known if anything affected it towards an improvement or had an opposite effect. It played havoc with my brain.

However, after that came something that changed my life, and all for the better, and it was the idea that I am my own cheerleader. Yes. It might sound ridiculous, especially coming from someone with such a severe disposition. But there is power in these words, that you can be your own motivator, an inspiration to your own self. I did not start out as someone I ever thought would be motivated, but I became that, I became someone to cheer for and someone who could cheer all the same.

I guess nothing in my life that led me to becoming that can be more important than my bipolar disorder, or rather, overcoming it. You see, a condition such as mine leaves you hopeless, primarily because of how it changes your life. I would go from a normal, everyday guy to someone who very much thought themselves to be the Lord and Savior himself, or someone who tries to communicate to the sky people because if he won't, bad things might happen. My worlds either turned upside down, or became something else entirely in these moments. Perhaps an even worst realization to gain from this is that these things often got told to me, and I pieced what I could from my thoughts after the fact. I do not know if what happened did happen exactly as I remember, or some distorted variation of it, or as something else entirely. This is the cruel reality that gets you. That you suddenly lose any sense of yourself, who you are, all in the span of a few moments, seconds, minutes, hours, days, who knows. The episodes could last a mere split second or last for a few weeks still. There was no way of knowing when they happened, for how long, and what form they took. I could be having an episode and nobody would notice. There is a hopelessness in that which I had to deal with, and it is exactly that hopelessness that left me worse for wear.

I would think to myself, that somehow, someday, my disease would be my end, that I would have to face the music without ever being able to hear it, that I would die not being me. That day never came, and has not yet, and I hope to God that it does not, letting me revel in my newfound realizations for a little while yet. You see, I finally found myself, my identity, amid the chaos of so many more. I am not saying that it was all in my head, but that is where it starts. If something tried to control me, I was not to just lay there and let it, but to try my absolute hardest to take the reins and make the best of the situation and circumstances presented to me. That is the idea. That you have to adapt, fight back if you have to, to either learn to live your life with it, or to try to master it. A bipolar disorder is something that may never be cured, but don't let that hold you back. Now you know the odds you are against. It is better than not knowing.

So I learned how to control it, in a sense. It started out small. For once, I stopped thinking about my bipolar disorder one day leading to my demise. Sure, I landed in jail, got myself in increasingly worse situations, but that would only mean that I would have to fix a few more things along the way. I tried my hardest to change, but not to change myself at once. I started with a small, almost trivial and unrelated change in my life. I started to forgive. You know how you are in traffic, see some other driver cut you off and just make some of the most idiotic decisions that human beings should never make. Well, you might be inclined to be enraged right at that moment. After all, you should be. And that is where I made my change. Sure, I had every right to be angry. But that emotional flare up is exactly what I wanted to avoid. I wanted my emotions to be under control. So, I forgave that person. They wanted to pass, I let them. I would arrive at my destination a few seconds late. But I would arrive calmly and safely, which is decidedly better than angry and still late.

I guess what I am trying to say is that a small change to make your life better can be a good start. Perhaps if my life without a bipolar disorder wasn't as chaotic as being caught driving under the influence and in possession of drugs on more than one occasion, I would fare better when I had my episodes. And it did exactly that. It changed me. It gave me control I never thought I could get. It starts small, and perhaps that is the secret, never really going to extreme lengths to seek change, but be subtle. It can really have quite the change, and it can really make you your own cheerleader. I slowly made it back to being myself again. I had a few false starts, where I had thought I was back to normal only to realize later that I hadn't been at all. I was no longer a lunatic, but I was addicted to Oxycodone.

You are your own greatest cheerleader. That's the main theme of this book. No matter how much they may try, your loved ones just can't help you out as much as you wished they could. When you realize this and begin to cheer for yourself it becomes easier to pick yourself back up each time you're on your knees. I've been there numerous times throughout my life and even more so since I've been diagnosed with bipolar disorder. Take small steps at first and you will start to notice changes.

If you do happen to have bipolar disorder too, bless your heart. It can get better for you just like it did for me. You have to get your medications straight. I am on a perfect dose of medication right now and no longer feel like a zombie. I don't realize any side effects for that matter. I haven't had an episode in three years now and I pretty much feel like a normal person. Calling myself normal is strange though, especially after telling you everything I have about myself.

I know how I come off in this book. I'm not a baboon or a junky. I'm just a regular person kind of. I've used drugs and I've self medicated and I'm not ashamed to admit it. I'm generally a happy person and I haven't had an episode in over 3 years now.

Despite having bipolar disorder, I was still able to accomplish a lot of things. I graduated college and have a degree in Business Management, I own a marketing company, hey, I wrote this book. You probably don't want to write a book, but maybe you do. If I can do it, you can do it. You probably can't become a successful rapper though. I'm just saying.

For the record, I am not a Stan, nor have I ever been one. I feel strangely towards Eminem and that's because I knew him before he was famous. I'm a fan. That's for certain, but I often wonder if I would enjoy his music as much had I never met him. There's a lot of his music that I don't listen to, but he's got a lot of really good songs. He's still Marsh to me and I enjoy watching his fame grow from afar.

You can view my photo albums online at album.hatesmile.com. The next book will be called Part II, so look for it if you crave more. Now that I know what goes into creating a book, it won't take me five years to complete the next one. Look for it at Christmas time at an Amazon near you. Until then, I'm on to the next episode…

www.ingramcontent.com/pod-product-compliance
Lightning Source LLC
Chambersburg PA
CBHW022201050726
47590CB00002B/603